Keeping Safe in a Dangerous Place

An essential guide for everyone

ISBN: 978-1499308136

Contents

This book is dedicated to the special ones taken before their time.

Keeping Safe in a Dangerous Place
An essential guide for everyone

Introduction

In the late nineties I lived in Central America for a couple of years. I had already been a Krav Maga unarmed combat instructor for more than a decade and had experience in dignitary protection and counter-terrorism security as an operator and instructor. Together with a select group of skilled people we ran specialist courses and provided consultancy for high net-worth individuals, corporations, security personnel, business executives and their families, government ministers, as well as some people from other interesting walks of life. We trained people from Guatemala, El Salvador, Honduras, Costa Rica, and Mexico.

Violent crime was a way of life in that region and kidnappings, murders, executions, gang rapes and robberies happened literally on a daily basis. The president of one these countries brought in an expert to try and take control of the kidnapping epidemic and he requested that we write a special course for people at risk of kidnap, or for people who had been kidnapped who were likely to be re-targeted.

This particular course was mostly classroom based, with a few practical exercises thrown in. Depending on the level of interaction with the participants the course could last anywhere from 8 to 12 hours. It was fairly intense but enjoyable. People laughed on it. People cried. But everyone left having understood the basic lesson that the world is not a safe place, and you have to look out for yourself because no one is looking out for you.

This guide can help keep you from becoming a victim. From being attacked, from being hurt and from being traumatised. Obviously you cannot defend against everything but with a little knowledge you can avoid much of the day-to-day violence that you hear about in the news.

This book is relatively short and is written in every day English. Some of the sections are self contained and can be read in isolation however there are principles and tactics throughout that are not repeated in each section and you will gain a more comprehensive understanding of how to keep safe if you read the whole book.

From a content point of view I believe it is suitable for everyone from a mature high school/secondary school student upwards. It is for men, women and children; for travellers, students, and executives – we are all at risk from the same types of crime and you will learn practical, common sense tips and advice for keeping safe in different environments and situations.

I hope you enjoy it, find it helpful, and that it leaves you more aware than you were before you read it. Crying is optional.

Oscar Leon

London, 2014

Threat and Risk Recognition

Are you at Risk?

Yes, you are. We all are. This is not me scaremongering – you have already bought this book (I hope!) and I am not trying to sell you anything else off the back of it. The fact that you are reading this makes me think that for some reason you are concerned for your safety. Either something bad has happened to you, or you know someone that something bad did happen to, or you are about to embark on a new chapter in your life and need some security tips, or you are just being proactive because you understand the dangers.

The first thing that we need to understand is that there is no such thing as one hundred percent security. But, there is so much that we can do to mitigate the risks we face that we can dramatically increase our chances of staying safe.

The world is not a safe place. It does not matter which country you are in. There are always unpleasant, violent sociopathic people around. Some countries of course are far more dangerous than others. Sometimes the violence may be linked to a particular city or neighbourhood, but in general, every place has the same crimes, just some more prevalent than others.

Obviously high crime rates are linked to areas with higher levels of poverty, but it also depends on the strength and ability of local law enforcement. I say this because I firmly believe that many people have a predilection towards crime, and it is only the fear of consequence that prevents it. Most people do not want to go to prison; do not want to be arrested; do not want the humiliation of friends and family finding out what they have done.

Crime against you is likely to happen when you least expect it. You will be going about your daily life unsuspecting, when suddenly you are attacked. There are some countries in the world, thankfully a minority, where you can go into any high school and ask 16 year old students if any of them know someone who has been raped, robbed, car jacked, kidnapped or killed, and worryingly most people put their hands up (and it's not because they all know the same person!).

If you become a victim of one of these types of crimes, the worst case scenario is that you will be sexually assaulted, crippled or killed. In most cases you may just sustain a few minor injuries and lose some money and valuables. In all cases you will suffer extreme emotional distress and loss of confidence. By being prepared we can avoid much of this.

You need to give some thought towards the kind of mentality a person would need to possess in order to prey on innocent people. To understand how the violent criminal behaves you have to step outside your normal frame of reference. Attackers are not like you. They are not nice people. They go through life looking for opportunities to attack innocent members of the community. They have no qualms about causing suffering, pain, injury and death. They have no ethics and they have no morals.

This book does not address the psychological behaviour of violent criminals but if you are interested in reading about it I can recommend "The Gift of Fear" by Gavin de Becker.

For our purposes, what is important to understand is that most attackers do not like to fight. They look for quick and easy opportunities. They do not want to be caught, have their name in the news, and go to prison. They want their victims to be just that: victims. You are not going to be that victim.

How to be an Easy Victim

An easy victim? You might be thinking "Why would I want to be a victim at all, never mind one that makes it easy for my attacker?" Exactly!

There are lots of different types of crimes involving violence. We can list (but not limited to): bullying, kidnapping, mugging, murder, rape, and robbery.

Depending on the criminal and the situation, a robbery could lead to rape or murder. A rape could lead to robbery or murder. A mugging could lead to rape or murder. Maybe all these crimes were committed by someone who started his life as a bully and decided to graduate to something more serious.

Rape and murder victims often know their attackers. For the moment, let us talk about random victims of crimes. Or rather I should say, let us talk about you being attacked by someone you do not know. To say that you were attacked randomly is technically a misnomer because in many cases it was not random: you were chosen because you met the attackers' requirements. You fitted the profile the attacker was looking for and you entered the chosen "kill zone" at the right time.

So what was it about YOU that caused you to be chosen over someone else? The answer is simple: you were perceived to be an easier target.

Read the two scenarios below. Imagine you are standing near a bank at night. The area is virtually deserted and it is raining.

A young guy approaches the bank. You can see headphones trailing up to his head, which is covered by a hood to shield him from the light rain. His head is angled downwards and he is lost in thought, listening to his music. He goes directly to the cash machine, withdraws his money and walks away with it in his hand before starting to stuff it in his wallet.

In the second scenario the same young guy approaches the bank. As he approaches the bank he pulls down his hood. You see him remove his headphones. He scans the area as he goes towards the cash machine. He puts his card in, checks again no one is close to him then taps in the code. As the money is despatched from the machine he takes it, scans again the area, files it in his wallet whilst still facing the cash machine, puts his wallet away and then walks off, once more scanning the area.

Which one of those people would you rush up to, punch, threaten and steal the wallet from?

I am hoping that you chose the first guy. Why? Because he was completely unaware of his surroundings and he made an easy target. He was listening to his music. His peripheral vision was restricted. He had no idea of personal safety. He would not have seen the approach. The second guy was simply a harder target.

So what is the fundamental difference between an easy target and a hard target? Awareness.

Awareness

For an unknown person to make a successful attack against you they generally need surprise. Criminals rely on shocking you into submission. This could be by being verbally aggressive and threatening. It could be by a sudden physical assault – which could be a prolonged vicious attack or just a couple of slaps around the face to cause intimidation. In most cases it would be a combination of verbal plus violence.

I will re-iterate the above because it is the most important aspect of self protection. Whether a mugging, a robbery, a rape or a kidnapping, the assailant(s) require surprise in order to be successful. I will elaborate on this further on in the book.

What do we mean when we talk about "awareness"? Well, awareness can be defined as "consciousness of your environment and the knowledge of what things to look out for."

For our benefit, there are four colour coded levels of awareness. These help greatly to explain the levels of alertness you should be employing when you are out and about.

Condition White – total lack of awareness

Condition Yellow – 360 degree environmental awareness

Condition Orange – identification and evaluation of threats

Condition Red – fight or flight decision.

Ninety-five percent of people are in condition White 95% of the time! This means that they cannot detect any pre-incident indicators.

Some examples of condition White would be: leaving home in the morning without scanning the area before you actually close your front door behind you. Getting into your car whilst completely oblivious to the world around you; not checking if anyone is lurking nearby on foot or in cars or even on the back seat! You drive to work or take the kids on the school run and do not remember anything about your journey because you were driving on autopilot with no idea what vehicles were behind or in front of you. This is the reality for most people wherever they live.

Condition Yellow is the level we should all be at as often as possible. It is the exact opposite of Level White. We want to be situationally aware; to know who and what is around us. Obviously it is quite difficult to maintain this all the time – but with practice you can learn to increase your observation skills at key times.

Condition Orange is the mental state you increase to when you identify a potentially threatening situation. These are generally simple things such as you're leaving your house but see a stranger lurking near your car. Or you are walking down the road and see a group of unruly people acting with some level of aggressive behaviour, or you are walking away from a cash machine when you notice someone make a bee-line towards you.

Condition Red is the next elevation of the mental state where you recognise you are in trouble – that there is going to be violence – and you need to decide whether to try and fight it out or escape to safety. I will go into more detail on this in later chapters.

You may have noticed from the Awareness Chart that we are not just talking about situational awareness. Levels White and Yellow deal with knowing what is going on around you, but levels Orange and Red are about adjusting your mindset to the fact that you are getting closer to having to react, or that you have to react.

The original Colour Code system was devised by Jeff Cooper, a former US marine and nationally recognised combat weapons instructor. His Cooper Colour Code, however, was not designed for situational awareness. It related to your mental preparedness for combat.

Although this book is predominantly about "tactics" and not combat "techniques", I think it is important to understand the mindset behind Cooper's system – it definitely is a valuable tool that can help you develop a stronger resolve. You can read about Cooper and his Code by searching online but in essence:

Cooper's level White was being so unaware that should you be attacked, you would be killed; not just because you wouldn't see it coming but because you left your home that day without the understanding that you might be attacked.

Level Yellow was walking around knowing, anticipating, that at some point you might be attacked, so you were psychologically prepared for such an encounter. This ties in with what I wrote earlier: if you cannot be surprised easily then you are a much harder target.

Level Orange is simply the next stage up whereby you have identified a possible threat, the likelihood of an encounter is that much closer, and mentally you take that deep breath and are prepared to engage if need be.

Level Red – having prepared to fight if need be in Level Orange...the need is be!

We now know that we must be aware of our surroundings as much as reasonably possible. To help achieve this we need to increase our skills of observation.

Observation Skills

We all walk around every day without paying attention to what is going on around us. We are busy, have lots of things on our minds and are constantly stressed. But as mentioned, we need to be aware of what is happening around us – we need to be in Level Yellow as much as possible.

How many times a day do you absent-mindedly look at your watch but if someone then asks you the time you have to look again at your watch? This is looking without seeing. We all do it. Not just with our wrist watches but in lots of things. You can look behind you whilst walking down the road but if asked how many people were within a 5-metre range you would not know.

To help "see" when looking there is a method you can introduce called "commentary walking". Commentary walking is quite simply giving a running commentary about what you are seeing around you, for example, "Man in twenties walking toward me wearing blue jeans, black boots, green jumper and brown jacket." Typically, this is done silently in your head but you could also murmur it to yourself if that helps; just be aware that it may look a little strange to the people around you!

You might think that this is a hugely time consuming task but in reality it is not, and you adapt very quickly to doing it as part of your routine.

There is also "commentary driving" for when you are in the car. Advanced motorists and police pursuit drivers are taught this technique for identifying potential hazards in every day driving.

The more commentary walking and driving you do the more you will take in your surroundings and you will without a doubt start to notice when things are out of place, or situations that pose a potential threat. To give you a very simple example, with your new found awareness imagine you are walking towards your High Street bank and as you approach you see a guy with a heavy coat leaning against the wall, apparently doing nothing. At the same time you notice a car parked illegally outside the bank, with the driver in the car and the engine idling.

These two people may not be linked. The guy against the wall may just be waiting for someone to pick him up, but it is strange that he has chosen that particular place to stand. The driver may be waiting for his pregnant wife to come out of the bank.

In your new world of suspicion though, the two are linked. The people there probably have nothing to do with you but your suspicions lead you to think that the man against the wall is a spotter for the (unproven) robber currently inside the bank, and the car and driver are for the getaway.

All those thoughts went through your head in about the time it took you to take 3 or 4 steps. You then have a few more thoughts. Maybe the guy in the street is waiting to abduct someone coming out the bank, using the car and driver to get away. Or maybe the man against the wall is just waiting to grab some cash from someone making a withdrawal from the cash machine. Maybe the driver is really just waiting innocently for someone, as is the man against the wall.

So what do you do? For all the above scenarios it does not seem conceivable that you are the target (unless you are routinely in that place) but that does not mean that it is safe for you to be there. If you did withdraw cash from the machine you would be potentially volunteering to be a victim if your theory about the man standing against the wall is correct and he is a mugger. Alternatively, if there was a bank robbery going on, or some other serious crime, you would have placed yourself right in the middle of it.

So, do you ignore all these thoughts and continue into the bank or do you continue walking past for a few metres, perhaps glancing inside the windows as you pass by, and stop a safe distance away to evaluate? I am a firm believer that if you have noticed something out of the ordinary, that you should take precautionary measures. These precautions may only delay you for a few seconds or a couple of minutes but they could be the difference between you becoming a victim and you keeping safe.

In the bank example above, you can simply walk past the bank, glance in as you pass the front, and try and see if anything suspicious is going on. You can stop one or two stores away and observe the bank, the suspicious guy and the suspicious car. You could possibly cross the road if it gives you a better perspective and if you feel the need. Alternatively, or at any time during this process you can just decide to completely leave the area and go to another branch, or come back later in the day.

When we conduct our Security Awareness & Attack Recognition courses we often have an assistant hang around the car park where the course attendees will park. It is this persons' role to get close enough to the attendees that they can be seen. The attendees do not know this person. Our assistant might walk past one of them parking their car, may shadow someone else into the building, brush past them in the lobby, or even take the same elevator, sometimes also taking surreptitious photos.

At some point before lunch, after we have spoken about *awareness* and *observation*, we ask the attendees how aware and observant they think they are. Some will say not very, whilst others are proud of their skills.

We then bring in the people we used earlier in the day and ask who has seen them before. No one ever has. The assistant then describes where he was earlier, the proximity to the attendees, what information he picked up, and shows the photos. This is a very simple exercise that makes people realise how they look but do not see, or in fact in most cases, do not even look!

When you are out and about in the routine of your daily lives, play a little game. Imagine a friend of yours is trying to follow you. That at the end of each day you will get a photo and a report of how he or she followed you from your home to the tube, walking just behind you on the opposite side of the road but you did not notice. In your mind, it's your job to detect that person – to know when and where they are following you.

I am not saying that you should become paranoid and start checking dustbins and post boxes for people hiding inside them, but a healthy sense of awareness, being in Condition Yellow, will make you far less of a potential victim and a harder target.

Suspicious People

Now that we have an understanding of awareness and observation we can talk about what makes someone appear suspicious.

Our definition of a "suspicious person" is anyone (any age, gender, or race) whose appearance in your area attracts your attention, and along with your "gut feeling" you decide to treat them as suspect and act accordingly.

Security people are trained to detect suspicious people, usually for criminal or terrorism concerns. But whether a terrorist or a mugger, a kidnapper or a car thief, the characteristics we need to look out for are the same.

Unusual Appearance: The person could be showing signs of nervousness or agitation. His face could be flushed without apparent reason, or his skin unduly pale. He could be sweating whilst it is cool out, or trembling, or just generally acting as if he has something to hide.

The person could look out of place for his environment. I do not really want to get into the debate about racial profiling, but if you see a white person pull up in a vehicle in a predominantly black or Asian neighbourhood then he will stand out.

There could be signs of unusual behaviour compared to the norm for that location or area such as the person is standing still whilst others are just passers-by. The person may be noticeable because he is on his own and everyone else is in groups. He

13

may be standing whilst everyone else is seated, or paying attention to a particular direction when no one else is.

Unusual Presence or Movement: Someone who hangs around a particular place for a long time without apparent reason is suspicious. For example a man is still waiting at a bus stop even after all the buses that stop there have been and gone at least once. Obviously there are many legitimate reasons why this may have happened, but until proven otherwise it should be treated as suspicious. Equally, if someone tagged as suspicious, or even if not, leaves an area and then returns, especially if they have changed clothing or added a bag to change their appearance slightly, then that is suspicious too.

If someone is waiting in an area where there is nothing to wait for. Imagine walking down a road where there are just walls on both sides, and someone is randomly leaning against a wall; you have to wonder what possible reason there is for being there.

If there are queues to enter a venue because security are searching or profiling (could be a club, shopping mall, airport, or anywhere with security), a suspicious person may be evaluating which line is moving quicker and change lines based on the likelihood that the security for that queue are not being as thorough. Similarly a suspicious person may move towards the back of the queue due to nervousness or just because he is banking on security getting tired and lax as time passes.

A person's dress may not fit in to the environment. It might be a warm day and he is wearing a coat, or gloves, or a hood that hides his face. These things tend to stand out because they are not normal. Someone could be dressed very casually but it is a business district where everyone is suited, or it could be a black-tie event. Wearing sunglasses when it is overcast; not everyone is a pop star!

If you were standing outside a bank and three people march in carrying long, heavy bags or holdalls, it should ring alarm bells. Yes, they could be workmen carrying tools, but they could also be carrying weapons. Any bag that seems unduly heavy for its size, or is particularly long, or has strange bulges could be deemed as suspicious. Following various suicide bombings the general public is now more aware of suspicious people with backpacks, but as with all suspicious people and objects, if we are honest it also comes down to the profiling of the person.

Covert contact between seemingly random people should definitely raise your suspicions. Also, look out for people similarly dressed, or with the same physical characteristics possibly carrying the same types of bags.

I can tell you with some certainty that if you stood in the street watching a particular stretch of road with the usual smattering of banks, coffee shops, restaurants, office buildings and grocery stores that within not much time you will have identified some suspicious people. You will think that there can be no plausible explanation for their "suspicious" behaviour. The person is definitely a mugger, a kidnapper, a paedophile. But, most things that look suspicious usually do have an innocent explanation. But not everything!

In the world of self protection it is normal to have a lot of false positives – where something or someone has been identified as potentially suspicious that then proves to be harmless. This is no bad thing because it is better to be aware of potential threats and keep an eye on them, rather than not seeing them in the first place. With some practice you will be able to determine quite quickly what remains suspicious, and more importantly, what is of potential concern for your own well being.

Always listen to your gut feeling. Even if you have no tangible reason for having your suspicions, if something has caused you concern, even if you cannot identify what or why, proceed with caution. Your subconscious mind often picks up on things that the conscious one has not yet processed.

If you do see something suspicious, it is often human nature to discount it as nothing serious through fear of actually confronting the issue (mentally or physically). "I know I saw that guy two mornings in a row near my house, and now in the Starbucks near my office, but it is probably just a coincidence..." Most people do not want trouble, do not want to acknowledge trouble, and will find ways to write it off. Try not to dismiss suspicious activity until you have logged it or ascertained whether it really is suspicious or not.

Threat and Risk Recognition Conclusion

Up until now we have spoken primarily about awareness and observation, the two key attributes that form the basis of self protection; tools that will make you more aware of your surroundings, and help you to identify potential threats. Identifying a potential threat does two things:

1. In most cases it will cause the attacker to disregard you as a target. He will know you have noticed him and therefore he has lost the element of surprise.

2. It mentally prepares you for a potential attack, and gives you the time and distance to react or to extricate yourself completely from the area.

Hopefully, you will have now started to relate a little to some of the tactics and concepts that we've discussed, and realise that if you exist day to day in a Level White condition that you are making yourself vulnerable to attack and will not be mentally prepared to react positively.

The scope of this book is limited to self-protection tactics, not fighting techniques. But when we talk about "positive reaction" we mean taking decisive and aggressive steps in order to make yourself safe. This could be extricating yourself from the situation by guile and speed or it could mean fighting your way out.

I would have liked to include fighting tips in this book that could help you in a violent encounter but the reality is that reading about techniques is almost as useless as training in a class that doesn't permit striking or contact, or that doesn't pressure test the techniques in close-to-real-life-situations.

To learn how to fight you need to train hard. You need to find an instructor that runs regular classes or courses that cater to self defence or combatives. In my opinion Krav Maga is probably the best self defence system available however I would research your instructor carefully, and observe or participate in a class before you commit. In recent years there has been a commercial explosion of schools popping up all over the world under the auspices of the various legitimate and not so legitimate Krav Maga organisations. Some instructors will be good, some may well be incompetently bad, some mediocre and on rare occasion you will find great ones. Try to find the great ones. There are undoubtedly other instructors out there with their own combative systems that are also worth looking at but for the uninitiated they might be hard to find.

My final comment on this section before we move on to specific tactics for more defined situations is this: I work on the premise that everyone is out to do me harm until proven otherwise. Obviously I am not referring to people I know or encounter during the normal structure of day to day living (relatives, friends, store attendants, business people), but people who suddenly appear on your radar whose presence is not easily understood or their reason for being there is not clear. That might sound a little extreme but in reality it is not and it is the only way that you can maintain a level of awareness that will have any meaningful benefit to your safety.

PRACTICAL SAFETY TACTICS

The following sections provide you with situational tactics that will help you keep safe during regular day to day activities.

Security in the Street

Projecting Confidence

The way you present yourself is vital. Looking timid or nervous attracts attention, especially to criminals who are looking for victims. When walking through an unsafe area or in a location you are not familiar with you should always try to walk with confidence. You belong there. You are not lost, or confused or unsure of your surroundings. You know where you are going, and you know how you are going to get there.

When passing people who make you feel intimidated, the same thing applies. Bullies thrive on fear. Do not show concern. Do not acknowledge them. Focus ahead, either to your destination or to your imaginary friend waiting a short distance away.

A friend of mine has a tactic for when she is feeling unnerved by someone nearby. She often goes for walks in public parks by herself, which should be a safe thing to do in London during daytime but you can never be sure if there is a rapist lurking around, someone from the local hospital asylum who has not taken their medication, or just a general low-life. So if she is unsure, she will pull out her phone as if answering it and say "Where? Oh yeah, I can see you; 2 minutes". Or without the phone, she will wave to an imaginary person in the distance.

Both the above small acts can cause a potential attacker to pause just enough to give you sufficient time to walk far enough away that you have now become an unviable victim. Obviously, if there is no one at all visible within the horizon the attacker may notice that and may not fall for your guile.

It is also a good idea in such a situation that, if you know where the closest exit is, or group of people, or cafe, that when you "answer" your original imaginary call or even make your imaginary call, that you change direction and take the shortest but most public route to that location. Do not continue on with your walk if you suspect that someone maybe following you or lurking around.

It is important that you pay attention to your intuition. If you feel uncomfortable or concerned then there may be good reason why, even if that reason is not immediately apparent. You may have subconsciously noticed something about that person. He may be carrying a bag that did not suit the environment, or has a dog lead to help him blend in but you had not seen a dog anywhere on your walk.

Of equal note, it is important to not put yourself in potentially vulnerable situations in the first place! Do not take that short cut down the alley. Do not cut through the deserted or sparsely populated park whether day or night. Think if you were a mugger or a rapist where you would prey, and be wary if you need to be in such a place.

Clothing and Jewellery

Wear suitable clothes for your destination. Give up pride and glamour for safety. For women, flat shoes are more practical. Do not expose expensive jewellery.

OK, that may be straightforward and common sense, but obviously it is a lot easier to say than it is to achieve, especially in a normal city environment. Unless of course you are living in, or travelling to, a country or city that is renowned for street robberies and violent crime. I do not want to single out any specific countries but if for example you were walking the streets of Sao Paulo, Brazil, or Johannesburg, South Africa, I am quite sure that you know not to be wearing your Rolex or Cartier watch or showing off that shiny diamond ring.

You might be reading this and thinking to yourself, "I am not going to let some scumbag thief cause me to live my life differently to the way I want to live it". Yes you are. I mean, yes, you are probably thinking that and yes, you are going to let the very valid and real fear of violent crime cause you to dress according to the environment you are in. Because you do not want to lose your valuables and you most certainly do not want to get hurt.

If you are living in a big city in the Western world, it should not be a problem driving your luxury saloon, high end 4x4 or sports car on a daily basis. There are so many of them that no one pays attention, unless of course you go to a known poor area or violent neighbourhood. In that situation I am sure you will have given some thought to your clothing, to your jewellery, and to where you can find a safe place to park your car to stop it from getting broken into or stolen. The same thing will apply when travelling by public transport – although again, it will often depend on which areas you are travelling through. Not forgetting the walking at each end of your journey.

Women more than men are likely to be sexually assaulted due to the way they dress. Again, it will depend on the location. If a woman is wearing a figure hugging dress and high heels and looks quite sexy – in my opinion it would not be wise to be walking the streets alone at night. Do not for one moment think I am being sexist, or saying that women should dress more conservatively because that is not the case. But there are people out there who are looking to rape. There are people out there who, just like an opportunistic burglar will lean through an open window and steal a wallet or laptop, will see a "sexy woman" in the street walking past a park in the dark late at night, or secluded low populated area in the day, and a caveman thought of domination, sex, and lust could cause them to act on that impulse. Thankfully this is rare. But it is only rare because most women are wary and cautious about travelling alone at night. Most of the rapes you get to read about in the news happened at night, in low population areas, and quite often when the women's senses and awareness were impaired due to alcohol after an evening out.

In concluding this short but important section, dress according to your environment; blend in. Be the grey person. Let someone else be attacked instead of you. Consider taking a bag with a change of clothes for going home after a party, or for going home late from work. Replace your heels with flat shoes so that you can run or manoeuvre if you have to, or to even walk faster... how many women wear high-heeled shoes knowing they can only walk about 100 metres before they cannot go any further! Remove or hide your jewellery if you know you are going to have to travel through bad parts of town or if you are holidaying in a country that has a history of muggings or street robberies.

I have heard it said many a time: "I will not take off my ring for anyone." Although I think this attitude is more typical in the older generation, my answer usually is: "You won't have to – they will cut off your finger with the ring still on it."

The Arms-Length Principle

We now know that we need to walk with confidence, like we belong and are not intimidated, and ideally if we are in a bad area we will be dressed accordingly and not stand out.

We will now look at a few simple principles that can further keep you safe in the street. These principles are more "tactics" than "techniques," although there is a bit of both.

Generally when walking in the street you should be walking on the side of the road with the vehicular traffic coming towards you, not approaching you from the rear. Most people seem to know this but it is attributed to pedestrian road safety only, so that you can see oncoming traffic and not get hit from behind.

25

It is actually a similar principal from a security point of view. You want to be able to see who is approaching you, and you do not want a car to be able to sidle up behind you so that someone could jump out and attack you or abduct you. It is all about giving yourself time and distance in which to react.

When walking, scan your environment. This should be done in a relaxed surreptitious way; not like a chicken jerking its head around constantly. Watch out for alleyways or darkened areas such as openings to parks, cemeteries, forecourts to industrial units; places where someone could quickly force you down or drag you to without anyone noticing. Avoid such areas.

If you see someone that piques your concern, or a gang of unruly people, or a few guys standing by a wall with cans of beer in their hands, it will be appropriate to cross the road before you reach them. This is something you should do as soon as possible, before you get close enough for them to become eagerly aware of you. You should try and do this with a semblance of nonchalance; that you were going to be crossing the road anyway. Always try to take these actions in a relaxed way. If the potential attackers sense that you have crossed the road to avoid them it may anger them, and they could follow you or try to intimidate you by crossing the road and engaging with you.

In the above scenario, if you did not see these people with sufficient time to cross the road and avoid them, you have two simple options. One is to ignore them, focus ahead like we have already mentioned previously, be confident and just walk on by. The alternative is to stop suddenly, pat your pockets as if you have just realised you have left something at home, turn around and walk back the other way. You could potentially pull out your phone and make a fictitious call to that effect. This could diffuse a potential situation quite easily because the "attackers" will not feel slighted or insulted by your actions. But obviously you will now have to find another route to your destination!

Instead of hugging corners, take corners wide. You will be able to see more of what is immediately around the corner, on either side of the road if you are not butted up to the corner when you make the turn. If there is something there that you do not like then you can continue on past.

I know that most women already know this, but keep your handbag or satchel fastened shut. This is obviously to avoid pick pockets and opportunists. As well as keeping your bag closed try to have the strap diagonally over your chest so that the bag is not going to be easy to pull away, and if it has a satchel style opening have that towards your body (even if it is slightly less convenient to access the bag). This will show you as a harder target to someone who might want to wrench your bag from you, or even someone who is evaluating you as a potential different type of victim, such as for rape.

It goes without saying that valuables should be kept hidden and as inaccessible as possible. If you happen to be carrying valuable documents or diamonds, or more money than normal, have it secreted on you somewhere. Most jackets and coats have internal pockets and there are always money belts and money holsters for wearing under your clothing.

If someone asks you the time as you are strolling down the road, always be aware that it could be a distraction. Apart from the fact that it is incredibly rare these days for someone to not have a watch or a mobile phone with the time, it is also very rare to stop a random person who is walking along at pace. In this situation, if the agenda is crime then it is likely that the person asking for the time wants you to stop in a particular spot so that his accomplice(s) can grab your bag or threaten you with violence to give up your valuables. Or even just pickpocket.

Firstly, do not ever stop where they want you to stop. There is no harm in continuing to walk on past them for a good 2 metres. During this time if you were in Condition White you should have gone straight to Orange, understanding that you may be getting involved in a physical confrontation, and start scanning the area for suspicious looking people; anyone loitering with attention focussed on you. If you were in Condition Yellow then hopefully you would already have a sense of your surroundings and you just step it up to Orange.

After scanning the immediate area, you stop, turn and face the person that addressed you from that distance of 2 metres or so. Look directly at them and also scan the area between you and them and behind them for accomplices. Visibly check that the person has no weapons in his hands. If a hand is in a pocket I would be concerned. All this should just take a couple of seconds. You can then give him or her the time and be on your way. Alternatively you needn't stop at all and could ignore them, or again without stopping just say "Sorry, I don't have a watch" or "sorry, my watch is broken".

What did the above achieve? It is quite common for muggers and street robbers, or any other type of person intent on violent crime to disarm your inbuilt security features with a seemingly innocuous question. It may not have been "Do you have the time" but could have been "Can you give me directions to x" or "Can you show me on my map how to get to y" or "Have you seen my child?" or any number of things.

They quite likely chose that specific spot because it is busy and therefore unlikely that anyone would notice any criminal activity, or because it is secluded, or because there is an alleyway or car park they can quietly force you in to. Whatever the reason, they wanted you in a particular "box" but you did not comply and ruined their plan simply by taking those few extra steps. By not being in their "box" they could not continue with their plan. And if they thought to come after you they will have realised that you are extremely aware and a hard target, and in most cases would ignore you to find an easier victim. If they did come, you now at least have time and distance to react.

If whilst walking in the street a vehicle pulls up alongside you and someone from within the vehicle calls out to you to come over, or gesticulates to come towards them, don't! Keep your distance. Do not approach the vehicle. If you are already close consider moving away from the vehicle to the further side of the pavement. Check behind you and make sure there is no one suspicious. By suspicious I mean someone who is going to approach you with a weapon (for example a gun, knife, or syringe) and force you into the vehicle. Consider walking back the way you have just come a few steps. It is harder for a car to reverse and follow you than to drive forwards.

Acknowledge the driver or person who asked the question if you feel inclined to do so. In most cases it will be a genuine request. However, your own intuition should tell you if there is anything suspicious.

Understand that if you are a child and walking alone, it would be very rare for any adult to stop along side you because whether legitimate or not, they would not want to cause you distress or appear suspicious to others. If you are a woman walking at night, scantily dressed or not, it would be rare for an adult to pull alongside you for the same reason as stated in the previous sentence. It does happen though, and it could be legitimate, but unless you are living in a very safe rural town where people do not lock their doors and strangers offer each other lifts....No! Not even in that situation is it acceptable for you to get in a car with a stranger.

The only time you may ever want to consider getting into a car with someone you do not know is if you are facing imminent danger and someone has stopped to help you, or you have flagged down a car for assistance. You need to evaluate the situation as quickly as possible and try and determine if the driver is genuinely looking out for your best interests. It is likely that jumping into a random car is going to be less of a danger to you than staying in the violent situation you are already in.

To Comply or Not Comply

In the unfortunate circumstance that you are confronted in the street by someone who is threatening you, either with a weapon or without, to hand over your purse or wallet, it may be that the safest thing to do is to hand over your purse or wallet. If you are travelling or operating in a city that is rife with muggings and street robberies you may do well to have a "give-away" wallet or purse with you. The idea is to take a spare wallet/purse and fill it with receipts, some loose change; some store cards that look like credit cards but that do not have your name on them, and some cash. Preferably small denominations and potentially in a currency that has little value, so that losing it isn't really going to bother you. It is unlikely that a robber will examine it too closely in your presence in the middle of the street, and it can save you from exposing your name and address and having to cancel and replace all your credit cards and other documents.

It is also an option to throw this wallet or purse either to the ground or behind the attacker, to create for yourself an opportunity in which to escape. Obviously, if your escape route is in front of you, and therefore behind the attacker, then throw the wallet over your shoulder if you have the presence of mind to do it, and if you feel safe enough to do that.

If there is a knife to your throat or a gun pointing at you, then in most cases you will be compliant and hand over your valuables (or "give-away" wallet) as that is the most likely course of action to keep you safe. Unless you are well trained or you feel that somehow you can take the upper hand, either psychologically or physically, then you will have to do what your attacker says.

In some cases you will be terrified, in others you will feel a sense of incredulousness; in others you might be angry; or you could just not even register it through shock. I can tell you that it is quite acceptable to feel morally indignant; to be angry; to think "How dare you try to steal from me?" But only you will know whether it is wise to resist or not in that specific encounter.

So, I have said that you should do what your attacker tells you to do in a street robbery situation. But there is a caveat to that. A very serious life saving caveat. Do not ever, ever, allow an attacker to relocate you from where you are to somewhere else. Not two steps into a shadow, not into a building, not down an alley, and most definitely not into any vehicle. Ever.

There is absolutely no good or healthy reason in the world for an attacker to want you to go somewhere else with them. It can only be because they want to rape, hurt or kill you, or exploit you in some other way. You may think I am exaggerating but think it through and you will come to the same conclusion.

Let us look at some scenarios. You are walking down the street and a guy comes up alongside you and puts his arm casually around you. It takes you a moment to realise what is going on – you are shocked and it takes you a second whilst you are thinking "What the hell is going on?" He has a knife or syringe in his hand, or tells you he does, and says "Just keep walking. I need your help for a minute. I promise you I won't hurt you, I just need your help".

I can tell you with one hundred percent certainty that in a situation like that you need to react as immediately as you can to get away. Pull away and run and shout, "Help, he is kidnapping me" or "Help, he is a rapist" or "Help, he has a knife." Create distance and attract attention to the assailant. Be wary of jumping into the closest car in order to escape just in case that car was your assailants' destination!

You might be thinking that the assailant might stab you; might inject the syringe. It is highly unlikely that he will. He was trying to be discreet and he was relying on surprise and the threat of violence to quickly overwhelm you to a state of compliance. Most attackers are not completely unhinged and do not want to be caught.

But, the reality is that whatever the attacker potentially could have done to you in a public street full of people, he would do far worse to you in seclusion. So even if there is a risk of being hurt, do not give a second thought to reacting and getting away, because you are unlikely to have another opportunity. In a worst case scenario and you are hurt, the chance of receiving professional medical attention whilst in a public place is extremely high compared to no medical attention after being abducted.

It is said that in the case of an attempted abduction you should try to escape within the first 7 seconds or the first 30 seconds. Where those specific timeframes came from I do not know, but they are a good rule of thumb. There are two main reasons why if you are being abducted or kidnapped that you should make every effort to escape immediately and not try to wait for a more opportune and safe moment.

The first reason is because you are most likely still in a populated area where, if you attract attention, someone may come to your aid or call the police. Quite simply, there are more resources available to you.

The second reason is that of "crumbling", as in Fight, Flight, Freeze or Crumble. In an attack or abduction scenario your first reaction could be to fight. Or it could be to run away. It could also be to fight back to create the opportunity for you to escape to safety. But in many cases, especially if the attacker has chosen his victim well, you might freeze.

Crumbling, however, is slightly different to freezing. With freezing you just do not react through immediate fear; crumbling is when you are justifying to yourself the reasons why you should not react, fight back, or try to escape. Due to your fear (the fear of being hurt) you will start to rationalise your reasons for not fighting back or trying to escape. "I know I could try to escape. But he might hurt me. I don't want to get hurt. He probably won't hurt me. He looks OK. There must be a simple reason why he wants me. Yes, I am going to be OK".

You can see the train of thought and how the victim became more of a victim as each thought progressed. In your subconscious you know you are not going to be alright but you allowed yourself to generate so much fear that you crumbled. How long would that have taken? Most probably it took mere seconds; at worst a few minutes. This is why it is important to make your escape as immediately as possible, especially if you are in a public place; so as not to allow the crumble effect.

The only caveat to that would be if you were completely outnumbered and in the kind of situation whereby it is clear you would not survive the escape attempt (for example surrounded by illiterate or militant gunman in a third world country). If you are working in such a country you most likely would have received training for these situations. If you have not, or if you are travelling to a potential hot spot for a holiday then it is worth researching some "What to do if you are kidnapped" tips online. There are some very simple principles that are worth understanding. Later in this book is a chapter about how to avoid being kidnapped but I do not go into detail about how to endure captivity; that topic is not within the remit of this book.

Fight or Flight

In the previous chapters we have focussed mostly on tactics as opposed to techniques. We have spoken about the need to escape certain situations. We need to understand however that any confrontation is potentially life threatening. We have all seen videos or heard on the news about a guy that was punched in the head in the street or nightclub and died when he hit the floor from a brain aneurism. Or the mugger who stabbed his victim in the leg as a threat, but severed the femoral artery by mistake, leaving the victim to bleed to death. These were unintentional deaths by criminals and thugs. But there are people out there who do want to intentionally cause you physical harm.

Tactics will only get you so far. For sure they will help avoid many different situations. But not everything is avoidable. Sometimes you may be physically attacked, or face a very aggressive and violent situation, and you will get hit and you may very well get hurt.

To deal with a violent encounter in most cases you need to fight. To defeat a single attacker, or have any chance of escaping a situation with multiple assailants you need to train in a fighting system, more especially if weapons are involved.

Some modern self defence systems such as Krav Maga teach the "stun and run" tactic, utilising various techniques depending on the attack or threat. For example, if faced with a knife wielding street robber demanding your cash, and for whatever reason you decide that you are not going to comply, the standard defence is to slap the knife hand away, kick the attacker in the groin, and run away.

Krav Maga practitioners at this point are jumping up and down with excitement saying "He mentioned Krav Maga again, and I know that technique and tactic". Hopefully they will also know that it is insufficient to teach solely that technique and tactic, and I will explain why.

Firstly, I have chosen this knife threat situation to outline several points – it is not an issue with Krav Maga, of which I have been doing the non-commercial version for more than 25 years. It is about the application when taught in isolation. What I mean by that is, if you go to a class and learn that particular defence you will feel empowered, but the reality is that if the instructor did not explain the bigger picture to you then you may well try that technique and get stabbed or killed.

I wrote earlier that it is not within the scope of this book to teach how to fight because it is not really feasible, and now you will see the difficulties of trying to explain techniques in the written form.

Imagine you are standing in the street, with your left foot slightly ahead of your right, in a loose fighting stance. Imagine the knife-wielding attacker in front of you, facing you, also in a left leg forward stance, holding the knife in his right hand. Your technique is based on him not suspecting that you will fight back; he is expecting you to be a compliant victim. With your left palm you swipe from left to right, striking his knife hand and slapping it towards the right, across the front of the attacker's body. You immediately execute a groin kick, either upwards with your instep or straight with the ball of your foot to his groin. You then turn and run to safety.

Where can this defence go wrong? Firstly, the first step of palming away the knife hand must be successful for the kick to work otherwise you are going to impale yourself on the knife. In the stress of the moment it is not easy to hit something the same width as your hand with your hand – it is a small target. Understand that the mugger may also be jumpy and retract his hand. That could work in your favour and it might also not.

The groin kick: it is not easy to access the groin with a meaningfully powerful kick; people generally do not stand with their legs astride in a horse stance. So you may have palmed the knife away and kicked, but the kick may not have had the desired effect. But you are so intent in completing the series of moves that you turn around and start to run.

But where are you going? I forgot to mention that it is night time, it's dark and you are in a secluded side street with no one around. You are unfit and overweight and the attacker is young, strong and fit.

So he has now caught you and stabbed you in a kidney.

My point is not that the defence does not work, because it can work. My point is that there are many variables and whoever teaches these techniques needs to also make his students understand what might go wrong. I highlighted this technique for two main reasons: 1) I wanted to show how much word space it took to explain a defence without even teaching how to do the actual techniques; and 2) I wanted, somewhat laboriously, to get to the point that running away is not always the answer!

If you do run, try to make sure you have a destination nearby; preferably somewhere that you can lock yourself inside (e.g. shop, car, residence). Of course, if you are a fast runner and your attacker is unfit then maybe you can outrun him, but running in a blind panic in an unfamiliar location is not always a good idea. Also, you must bear in mind that if your stun attack was unsuccessful, by the time you turn around to run your attacker could already be upon you, because he is already facing the right direction.

Therefore it may well be that you will have needed to attack him with more than just a groin kick in order to sufficiently incapacitate him to give yourself more time to escape. But that creates a whole set of different problems because you will now have to find a way to control the knife arm, which is very difficult to do when someone is actively trying to stab you multiple times either through anger or fear of their own. This is the reason why in situations like that it makes sense to give up your valuables and live to claim on your insurance.

I actually discussed this scenario recently with the current head of one of the Israeli Krav Maga global organisations. He shared my thoughts about the

39

diligence of the instructor building up the technique and pressure testing it in situations where it might fail but added that these techniques are designed for the "casual attacker" in public places; not the determined attacker that will hunt you down and kill you in a public place regardless of consequence.

Which brings me nicely to this very important adage: "The more I learn, the less I feel I know". If you do martial arts, self defence or combatives, and have done so for any serious length of time you will understand my point. Attackers do not conform to any rules of your training. The knife attack might not arc in the perfect way it needs to for you to execute that perfect block, trap and counter attack. The knife attack might be frenzied, repeated, from a person who is many times stronger than you, or dominating you by height, and/or on drugs. For me, my "attacker" is going to be the biggest strongest, fastest and most aggressive person I have ever come across. Which is an absolutely terrifying thought, but if I train for that, then hopefully anything less will be an encounter I survive.

Reviewing what we have learned in this section, we now know that sometimes it is better to give up your valuables when facing a weapon. That you should only run away if you have a realistic prospect of escaping and that if someone tries to move you from one place to another you should resist regardless of the consequences.

Which just leaves one remaining point: if you are physically attacked you will have to fight back.

If you do not fight back there is the possibility that the attacker or multiple attackers will become more frenzied. Bullies thrive on weakness and the weaker and more submissive you become the more violent and feral they are likely to be. So release the animal within, and fight back harder and more aggressively than your attackers. Find a reason to fight. Your reason may be so that you can get home and see your children or spouse, or so that you can go to work and earn a living, or just because you have no intention of letting a street thug take your life.

If you are out with friends and one of you is attacked, don't just stand there and watch, through curiosity or fear. You should make a united front and all of you should join in against the attacker. If there are two or three of you and just one attacker, it is far better for the two or three of you to try and neutralise the attacker rather than allowing the attacker to fight your friend, potentially hurting him, and then move on to you. Street fights are not fair. There are no rules. The attackers will do anything they can to win and you must do everything you can to stop them from hurting you.

Fighting Back

We learnt in the introduction to *Threat and Risk Recognition* that attackers (who potentially are just bullies) look for easy victims. Most of you will already know that if you stand up to a bully he will back down. In an attack situation, if you cower away you risk provoking a more serious attack whereas if you fight back, even though you risk getting hurt, you have more chance of causing the attacker to back away. Let us also not rule out that you could be a better fighter than he, or stronger, and could prevail.

If you do need to fight, be as aggressive as you can be. You do not know how far your attacker will go to win, so you have to go further and you have to get there first. There is no such thing as trying to "only slightly hurt" your attacker. You do not know what will hurt him and what will not, what will be effective against him and what will not. So you must use all your strength and aggression. Take the initiative and use surprise to your advantage. Hit first, hit hard, and keep on hitting until your attacker is sufficiently incapacitated so that you can make good your safe escape.

The "do-gooders" in the world will always say "you must not hit first" which is usually followed by "and you must only use minimum force". Obviously I completely disagree with the former as would do any person who understands these types of situations. You do not know whether your attacker's initial attack will knock you out, break a bone, strike a vital organ, or kill you outright. In my opinion, anyone who advocates that you should not use violence to defend yourself against attack is afraid to face reality and would like to hide behind their view that violence is reserved for criminals and people of lesser social stature than themselves. Clearly their argument holds no water, and if they were ever attacked I am sure they would want someone like you to be standing next to them to protect them.

Regarding the latter, I cannot stress enough – you are perfectly within your legal rights to defend yourself. If someone punches you, you cannot measure the percentage of force he put into the strike, do a quick calculation and retaliate with say 10% more strength. Imagine: he hits you, you try to hit back harder. He kicks you and you try to kick back harder. This is assuming he did not knock you down already. He stabs you and you stab him back harder. Except you cannot, because you are already lying in a pool of your own blood, dying. My point, as I stated previously: you do not know how far the attacker is prepared to go, and so you need to overwhelm him with your own attack, to break the flow of his attack by surpassing his aggressiveness with your own nuclear-powered aggression and relentless counter attack, and only then extricate yourself from the situation.

If you can pick up an improvised weapon, do so and use it. Again, the do-gooders will say you cannot pick up a brick, or an iron bar, or a bat, or a fire extinguisher, or a chair to use in your defence. Of course you can. And you will need to. Again, an unknown quantity has chosen to attack you. He made the decision for you – you need to fight for your life.

There are of course limitations to what you can legally and ethically do. If you have knocked your attacker out, or he is injured on the floor and you are in a dominant position, it would not be ethical whatsoever, if you then took a sharp edged weapon and stabbed him with it, or cut his throat, or inflicted additional harm upon him. It would not be correct to pick up a heavy piece of masonry and repeatedly drop or smash it on the unconscious assailants head. That would be murder. It is malicious. It is no longer self defence. If the guy is semi conscious and you are concerned he is going to get up and chase you then it would most likely be suitable to stomp on his ribs, to kick him in the head, to stomp on his ankle to break it. But again, to do all three may be seen as unreasonable force (depending on the circumstances) and you could be prosecuted. You should limit your counter attack to what you deem is reasonable and necessary at that time in that specific situation for you to escape safely.

It is however fair to say that if an attacker was using lethal force against you, and trying to kill you and he died in the process, you would most likely be exonerated. If the knife he was using against you was turned against him, and he died in the struggle, too bad. If a gun was pointed at you and you managed to grapple with the attacker and the gun was discharged into the attacker, intentionally or not and he died, too bad. If the attacker was strangling you to death and you picked up a brick and smashed him on the side of his head and he died, too bad.

Again, there is quite a simple logic behind it. You are being attacked and you need to do whatever you can to survive, as long as it is deemed reasonable.

Imagine a situation where an attacker is threatening to shoot you but you manage to strip the gun from him. You know how to use it, and you step away and try to control the attacker with the threat of force. He calls your bluff and pulls out a knife and advances on you. In that situation you have every right to open fire.

If however in the above circumstances you have control of the gun and you control the attacker, he complies and lies down on the floor, and then you shoot him...well, you know that is wrong!!

To clarify, if you are verbally accosted and you can walk on by and completely avoid engaging with the aggressor at all, then that is by far the best option. Ignoring the aggressor and not making eye contact may work and is obviously the favourable option.

If you are being threatened, or you are in some sort of dialogue with a potential attacker, there are those that say that you can "always talk a talker". If you have the ability to diffuse the situation verbally and walk away then great, do it.

But still be alert and prepared. Be in Condition Orange, ready to react and to elevate to Condition Red; to safely escape, or to fight and then safely escape.

Dialogue and Distance

In the *Arms-Length Principle* section we discussed trying to maintain distance between you and a perceived threat, whether that threat be a person or persons on foot, or in a vehicle. This is because for someone to attack you physically they have to be close enough to strike you, either with their arms, legs or head, or with extensions to their arms such as knives, bottles, chains, bats and iron bars.

Most attacks will start at close range, at talking distance. If a stranger stops you in the street to ask directions, or for any reason, you should always maintain a minimum distance from them. You should have sufficient distance between you to be able to see them at a glance from their head down to their hands. This is because if they are carrying a weapon and the use of it is imminent then it will be visible in their hands. If a hand is behind their back, or in a pocket, under their jacket or covered by a newspaper or article of clothing then that too should raise suspicions.

Distance gives you time to react. There is a saying that you may well have heard: "action beats reaction". In most cases, it is true. Which means the attacker will always have the upper hand if he is close enough to you.

To understand this better you can play a simple game with a friend. Stand facing each other, one arm's length apart. Have your hands open, palms flat against your thighs; your partner the same. You go first. The aim is to tap your friend on the top of the forehead, moving your hand as fast as possible.

You decide when to make your move. You will soon see that it is impossible for your friend to move away or deflect your hand. So that your friend doesn't feel too bad, let him have a go too.

You can then try the same thing with both of you starting with your hands being flat on your chest. It's a shorter distance for the hand to travel but it also allows the "blocker" to have his hands in a more favourable position to react (closer to the head). He still will not be able to block it.

What does this exercise achieve? It demonstrates that even in isolated test conditions, where the defender knows what to expect and therefore has the best chance of defending himself, that he does not have the time or distance to do so at that range. So understand that in a street situation, whereby you are verbally engaged by a potential assailant, possibly with distractions in play, that at normal talking distance you have pretty much no chance of avoiding being hit or stabbed, whether you are prepared or not.

When talking to someone in the street that is an unknown quantity you need to be more than one arm's length away from them. I mentioned earlier that you need to be able to see from their head to their hands within the periphery of your vision. In most cases to be able to do that you should aim to be at least two arm's lengths away; the further the better.

Understand that you are entitled to your own individual bubble of space, wherever you are. Standing too close is uncomfortable for all parties. The only reason a stranger would stand within arm's reach is either because they have no understanding of social etiquette, which is unlikely, or because they are trying to position themselves close to you, or draw you in closer to them for some nefarious purpose (punch, head butt, stab, slap), or simple intimidation.

For people who understand such things (through the practise of self defence or combatives) it is fairly standard when challenged in the street, or when talking to someone that you are concerned about, to half extend one or both of your arms out in front of you, and use them as a barrier or "fence". This is often done without even realising it.

The fence is essentially a fighting stance, but less rigid, and can be done in such a way that it appears non aggressive. Conversely, it can be used as an overt control mechanism - "STOP! Don't come any closer!" or "Back off!" or "Stay back!" For people who talk with their hands, or gesticulate a lot it might be an easier concept to adopt; for others it is something that needs to be practiced.

I said earlier that I want to avoid writing about techniques in this book as it is not really the correct medium for conveying such things, and it is really only through attending quality classes that you can learn. That said, if you already have some self defence or combatives experience then there are of course great videos that you can benefit from.

I am telling you this because if you want to understand the concept and techniques of "the fence" then you should look up Geoff Thompson. He has a comprehensive series of books and videos that cover various aspects of "real self defence". Geoff is the man that created a whole defence/attack system from the fence. This is information that is very much worth knowing.

Once the fence is up, once your hands are in position, they are there to ensure that the aggressor does not close distance on you, to get within range to execute a surprise and devastating attack. Do not collapse your fence. If the person moves towards you, then he walks on to your hands. You can step back slightly to create distance, but never reign in your arms as you are defeating the whole purpose of having put them up in the first place. Just be wary of someone grabbing them to pull you into them or to propel themselves into you with their punching or head-butt attack.

The fence is also a "positioning" tactic that in addition to helping you defend against someone closing the distance on you, and to help you defend against attacks from that talking range, it helps you position yourself, mentally and physically, to execute a range of pre-emptive strikes or counter attacks which we will briefly touch on in the next section *Fake Compliance*.

We now know how to maintain distance and also have an elementary understanding of the fence which hopefully you will look into further. In order to benefit from using the fence in real life you will need fighting techniques in your repertoire. Yes, the fence will give you the distance in order to react, and might help you control a situation, but if not then you will be in Condition Red and be fighting. I cannot stress enough, that real self defence and combatives can only be learnt in real life classes.

When I started this chapter I mentioned that an attacker will need to be close enough to you in order to strike. You may have noticed that I did not mention firearms. In a street robbery it is more likely that you will be threatened or attacked with a cold weapon (i.e. a knife) but in some countries being robbed at gunpoint is more common, and in fact it can happen anywhere.

In street situations the assailant will want to be close enough to you so that they can threaten you without attracting attention. We have established that with a cold weapon, it is harder to threaten you if there is distance between you. In most cases the same applies with a handgun. The gun will often not be in the attacker's hand – he may point to it in his waistband or not even show it to you at all, just threaten verbally that he has one. The biggest difference with a gun is that it can be used to control you from distance (although most likely not in a public place), and also to attack you from distance (shooting).

Dealing with a firearm in a robbery situation, as already mentioned, is the same as dealing with a knife. Give up your valuables. If you are well trained and know how to disarm someone then obviously that is an option but the risks are still very high, even if you have substantial training. Even if you are successful in disarming the attacker it is likely that a minimum of one shot would have been fired, and a loved one or innocent bystander could have been shot. Obviously, if you are in a situation whereby it is apparent that the attacker is going to shoot you then you have to do whatever you can to survive and just hope that neither you nor anyone else gets hit. Techniques and tactics for these situations can be learned in any good Krav Maga or combatives class.

Fake Compliance & Rape

If you are in a verbal encounter that looks like the precursor to a physical attack, then you have a right to make a pre-emptive strike in order to protect yourself. Pre-emptive striking is not necessarily an easy thing to do – it will require confidence in your chosen technique(s), and confidence for actually initiating an attack for which you do not know what the outcome will be. It is generally something you need to train repeatedly to be able to do.

What is the reason for striking your would-be attacker before he strikes you first? Purely and simply, it is to gain the advantage. Most people can sustain a few blows to the head before getting knocked down, before they are sufficiently hurt to stop fighting, or before they are knocked out, but that is not always the case and you do not want to risk getting hit at all if you can help it. So if a justifiable opportunity arises for a pre-emptive strike, then it should be taken.

But what is that opportunity? Will it present itself or do you need to create it? I will give a couple of examples below so we can understand the concept better.

You are somewhere minding your own business and a violent thug comes up to you, spits at you and says something along the lines of "I don't like your face and I'm going to fuck it up for you". That is a clear threat. You can cower away, try and talk your way out of it, offer to buy him a drink, wait for him to hit you and try and deal with it, or hit him first. He has shown his intent, physically and verbally and if it seems like there is no way out then you may want to consider a pre-emptive attack.

If you have already watched a video of Geoff Thompson's "fence" or other instructors teaching about confrontation, you will notice that before they make their devastating pre-emptive strike that they try to make the aggressor more susceptible to the strike by engaging their brain with a question.

Imagine someone standing in front of you, very aggressive, crazy eyes, salivating at the mouth, stuck in an anger loop saying "I am going to kill you". He will be tense and tightly coiled. It is hard to cause effective damage when someone is so wired. You are standing there with your arms and hands in some semblance of a fence. You ask an innocuous random question such as "Did you have lunch with my mum yesterday?" or "Did you see the football?" or whatever question you want to use. The idea is to engage the brain and cause the aggressor to think "huh?" This causes him to lose some of the tension in his neck and body which means your pre-emptive strike will be more effective. The pre-emptive strike should follow immediately after you uttered the question. The last word in your question is your pre-emptive strike trigger.

As I said above, this is something you need to train for repeatedly. Whether you opt for a single knockout strike to the jaw or unleash a flurry of devastating blows it is something that can only really be achieved by practise.

Subterfuge can work very well in helping you defend yourself. We have already discussed some simple nonviolent ideas earlier in this section and there is no reason why they cannot work in a violent encounter as well. Imagine you are in a bar and you are being threatened. Just before you are attacked you calmly look over your assailants shoulder and nod your head to the side as if to say "get over here", or with your hand you beckon over your imaginary friends. Most people will turn around to look, which is your opportunity to land your strongest accurate strike on the jaw or side of the head of your attacker. And then make good your exit. Do not hang around admiring your handy work. But also be prepared to follow up with as many other strikes as you need in order to subdue the attacker if your initial surprise attack was not as successful as you had hoped.

I believe that subterfuge can also work in certain rape situations. Rape is a very sensitive topic but this is a book about self protection and about not being a victim and I feel it would be remiss of me not to include some comments. Whether against men or women, rape is a horrific crime that generally leaves victims' traumatised. We have covered a lot of tactics about how to avoid getting in to such a situation but in a worst case scenario where you find yourself being threatened or attacked with rape you must try and fight off the attacker. It is documented that victims' who try to defend themselves, whether successfully or not, will be able to deal with the aftermath better than someone who just submitted.

I have said this before but it is important to repeat it: most attackers, including rapists, do not want to get caught. They need surprise and the threat of violence to subdue you. If you resist, scream, shout, struggle and fight back most rapists would be scared off. There is evidence to prove this.

As we are in the section titled *Fake Compliance* I will also add something that maybe somewhat controversial. If the circumstances of your situation do not allow you to resist, shout, struggle or fight back initially, you can consider pretending to comply with the rapist especially if it will stop actual physical violence against you and especially if you can see it leading to an opportunity to escape. "Please, I will do whatever you want, just don't hurt me". "Don't hurt me, this is actually a fantasy of mine, let's go somewhere quiet and more comfortable". Or whatever words you are comfortable saying.

If the rape is a result of lust and not anger then this subterfuge may particularly work. It is well known that men are easily manipulated by the thought of sex and showing your attacker a bit of fake attention may well give you some control and therefore opportunity.

If you can make an action that will result in the rapist putting down his weapon, and perhaps putting him in a vulnerable position such as with his groin exposed, you can use your hands or knees to strike that area repeatedly. You can even consider biting. As soon as the rapist is stunned, or preferably writhing around on the floor in agony, then make good your escape. If he did have a knife or weapon, try and take it with you. You can either keep it on you for self defence or throw it somewhere where he cannot get it like in a river, on a roof, or down a drain.

If he is on top of you, you can put your hands on either side of his face and push your thumbs into his eye sockets. You can bite his ear off. If you have something heavy to hand then strike him on the side of the head with it. If you do not have any improvised weapons and you have the angle to strike, you can cup your hands and clap them together over your assailants ears, which if done correctly will create a vacuum in his head and potentially blow the eardrum causing pain and disorientation.

Be aggressive, be powerful and be fast. Hurt him as quickly as you can. If necessary, make several strikes – blow his eardrums, attack his groin, poke your thumbs into his eyes; use an improvised weapon to stun him or knock him out. You want to ensure that you have sufficiently incapacitated your attacker so that you have time to safely escape the area completely. However, make sure that you do not get fixated on your counter-attack and forget to escape. You want to get away as quickly as possible.

I cannot stress enough, most rapists will not sustain their rape attempt if you resist with vigour. And if you are not in a position to resist initially then, as I have suggested above, you can use your wits and guile to perhaps create a situation that you can exploit.

Will Anyone Help You?

It is an unfortunate state of the world that if you are attacked you cannot assume that you can rely on anyone for assistance. Of course, people may come to your aid. There are always good Samaritans; people with a strong code of ethics who will face danger on your behalf. But the majority of time those people will not be around and those that are will be scared of getting involved; scared of getting hurt; scared of involving themselves in a conflict between different parties without knowing who is the victim, if indeed either are.

It is also often the case that people walking by would not have seen the build up of an altercation, so they only catch a glimpse of what is going on, and they may not understand the severity of the situation.

Safe Havens

This is more applicable for when you are travelling overseas or to unfamiliar places, however, even if you are currently in your "safe" city you should always give a thought to "where would I go if attacked; who would I call?". This is especially relevant for children who are out without adult supervision.

You should always try to plan where you are going, especially if you are in a country that suffers from high levels of violent crime, rape, kidnapping or terrorism. Know the area you are staying in. Know whether you can trust the police. If not, and even if you can, have a list of friendly nation embassies or consulates and know where they are and have their phone numbers tucked away on a card as well as in your phone. If you do get into trouble and you have escaped, or you feel you are being followed, it is important to have an idea where you can go to be safe, and not rush off in a blind panic.

Other safe havens could include shopping malls, universities, international hotels, hospitals, police stations and military bases; anywhere where there is security, although with Police and military locations it would depend on the country you are in.

Incident Awareness

Be wary of watching a scene unfold in the street. If there has been a terrorist attack somewhere, a stabbing, or a shooting, do not be part of the gathering crowd. Be the smart one and evacuate yourself from the area. Yes, you might be forfeiting that great video you could have uploaded to YouTube but should the situation escalate you will be caught in a stampede of panicking people, or the crossfire of a shoot out, or the explosion from the bomb the terrorist planted to kill the first responders.

Anecdotes

To conclude the section on *Security in the Street* I am including four short stories. The first is mildly amusing regarding road rage and bluffing; the second is a sickening account of a very violent encounter; the third is very short about a kick boxer who realised that martial arts do not really offer street self-defence capabilities; and the last one is a case study about a modern day "mugging".

The first anecdote is about a friend of mine, Alex, who had a minor road rage incident recently. He was driving in London when a cyclist on one of those tiny-wheeled folding commuter bikes jumped a set of lights and cycled right across the front of Alex's vehicle, causing him to brake hard. Alex, not being one to contain his thoughts very well, shouted some abuse at the cyclist. To be fair, most people would have.

The cyclist shouted back, pulled over, and dismounted. It was at this moment that Alex realised that the man was a mini giant; very tall and strong looking. According to him, the guy got off his bike to stand up, and kept on standing up! He stormed over to the car. Alex had opened the passenger side window and the cyclist leaned in and started being abusive. Alex, who always proclaims to be the innocent party, decided to get out and confront the cyclist face-to-face because he felt trapped in his car.

Alex is slim built, 5'10, 13 stone (182lbs, 83kgs) and in his late forties. Facing up to the cyclist he felt fairly small and insignificant. The cyclist took a step towards him with his fist clenched and arm pulled back ready strike. There was still some distance between them. Now Alex has done a reasonable amount of basic Krav Maga and understands the fighting mindset pretty well. He saw the size of the guy's fists and knew that going toe-to-toe with him was not a good idea. So he stepped forward into a casual fighting stance, hands and arms raised, and shouted at the cyclist in a slow and menacing tone: "Fucking come near me, and I will fucking hurt you". The guy stopped in his tracks, thought for a moment, then turned around, got back on his bike and pedalled away.

The primary lesson I want to highlight from this story is that a smaller guy scared off a bigger guy just by being confident and using the threat of violence. The reality is that no one wants to get hurt. The cyclist may have been a very tall, fit and strong guy, but he did not know the capabilities of my friend and realised it was not worth finding out. Just like a bully, when confronted he backed down.

The fact that Alex should never have exited his vehicle is something else we can learn from. We do not want to get into fights unnecessarily. The outcome could prove fatal. Alex did not want to fight – but he felt disrespected and wanted to prove his point, verbally. He was lucky though that the guy did not attack him. He was lucky the guy did not pull out a knife and stab him. He is lucky that he did not have to fight the guy and potentially hospitalise him and later find out that the cyclist was just a nice guy on his way home to his wife and kids who happened to have a minor road rage incident the likes of which happen every few seconds around the world. Neither of them were bad people and we need to try and stay calm in these situations.

The cyclist did not progress with his attack because Alex caused him fear, which is an important aspect of self defence. This book is about awareness and avoidance. But I have said that if you have to fight then you must be explosive and ruthless until you have neutralised your attacker(s) and are safe. However we have just highlighted a mid-ground; a tactic that may extricate you from the situation without having to fight: the psychotic bluff.

I wrote above that no one wants to get hurt. If you can convince your aggressor that they will lose and get badly hurt in the process then most people will back down. It often does not take much to strike fear into people. In my friend's case he gave the appearance of someone trained, and he swore and threatened violence. On the outside he demonstrated confidence but I can assure you that he was really quite scared.

Usually when you do that you also have to act a little crazy: use monosyllabic threats of violence; be wild eyed, salivating at the mouth, like a rabid dog. "Take another step and I will fucking rip your fucking head off you mother-fucking prick..." Make it as ferocious and vicious sounding as possible. It is an act designed to save you from violence so do not feel bad about anything you say; nothing is sacrosanct.

Maybe if you see that person again he will apologise and offer to buy you a drink. Maybe he too was just having a bad day. Of course he could just be one of life's scum and you will need to be careful.

Geoff Thompson calls the above "ballooning". It is obviously not something he invented but, as with the fence, he has analysed and perfected it. He also has some enlightening information on fear, and it is worth reading up the relevant books or watching a DVD.

***

My second story is about an attack I saw on some CCTV footage that I was showed just the other week. It was 10pm at night and a young man in his twenties was walking across an open car park that had a closed office building on one side and some flats on the other.

You see the guy walking across and then suddenly a man runs up and confronts him. Within about half a minute there are a further five guys surrounding the victim, standing approximately two metres away. One of the attackers suddenly whacks the guy round the front of the face or head with a bat. The victim immediately fell to the floor and then one by one each of the attackers, in a sickening and prolonged attack that lasted for approximately 90 seconds, hit the victim with a mixture of baseball bats and tyre irons.

The victim was lying on his side on the floor as if he were in bed, not moving and not protecting himself at all; not even in the default foetal position. You could see him twitching slightly with every strike. You could see the force of the blows. Luckily there was only one baseball bat and they were hitting him around the body and not the head. Twice one of the guys with a tyre iron had it fly out of his grip into the air with the force of the upward motion before he came back down to strike the victim.

Eventually the attackers ceased their physical onslaught and moved away from the victim. The victim, somehow still conscious and alive, miraculously stood up and started to stagger away. The assailants ran back, stripped him of his watch and wallet, and ran off. The victim walked out of shot but we know he collapsed about 20 metres away.

A few security professionals I know saw the video and concluded that there was nothing anyone could do in that situation. A couple of combative instructor colleagues of mine also saw it. We drew our own conclusions and we believe, partly because we have to, that something could be done in that situation.

Firstly, a physical encounter with even one person can be fatal, so with two or three attackers it is clearly far more dangerous. With more than three attackers it is rare for them all to attack you at the same time; there actually isn't the space for them to all get their strikes in together, at least not very effectively.

One essential aspect is to not allow yourself to be surrounded. A common tactic for these types of street gangs is to surround you, and whilst one is engaging you in conversation and causing a distraction, another will hit you in the head with a heavy punch or brick from the side, and then someone else will stab you, or attack you with fists, kicks, or bats. So keep your fence up and try not to get encircled. Keep moving.

If you have the confidence to initiate the attack then this is an option worth considering. It will create uncertainty to the attackers and if you can hurt one of them badly then do so.

If they attack first, you need to defend and counter attack immediately. The adrenalin will be flowing, your legs and arms may feel like lead, immovable, but once you get into a flow, you have a chance. If you can disarm one of the attackers, and get his bat, batter him senseless with it. Do not forget to always be scanning for incoming attackers – do not get tunnel vision when engaging with one attacker.

Then take the bat and attack another one of them. From a psychological point of view, you may wish to return to the first person you neutralised and stomp on him, or use the bat on him again; something that will cause the other attackers to further think that you are crazy; to create in them the fear of getting hurt; that you are going to hospitalise or kill them. Pause for a moment and tell them in a slow and measured tone "I am going to kill all of you". It might be a bluff, it might not be. They know as much how this situation is going to pan out as you do. Unless they are committed fighters or attackers with experience then many of them will just fold.

I am not saying that this is easy, and I am not saying it is survivable. No one knows. Every situation is different. The only thing I can tell you is that if you are still standing, still in one piece, then you have a chance. You have to change your mindset so that you are more aggressive than your attackers. Do not forget, they came in superior numbers, with weapons, and had surprise as an advantage. They were expecting an easy win; instant capitulation on your behalf. That has not happened. They need to re-evaluate. Hopefully they will leave. You can then go home, run a bath, light some candles...or more likely have a stiff drink!

YouTube is a wonderful tool. I found some videos by a combatives instructor called Branimir Tudjan, who is based in the Netherlands. I can tell you that from what I have seen of him he is one of the "great" instructors that I mentioned earlier (if you are looking for quality classes). He has all the correct attributes (not limited to): charisma, technical skills, teaching ability, experience, and humility. I would definitely spend some time watching some of his videos, or get to a seminar if it is ever feasible.

***

My third anecdote is about a comment someone made to me recently regarding a female kickboxing instructor who was mugged on her way home one day. The account is as told to me and is quite devoid of detail, but we can draw some good lessons from it nevertheless.

The woman was walking alone at night and was texting a friend on her iPhone. Two men came up to her from behind and tried to take her phone. She said that she found it really difficult to take on the two people and that she was lucky that she prevailed, but that they did get away with her phone and some other things.

You are probably wondering the same as me: in what way did she prevail because it seems to me that her attackers succeeded in getting what they wanted.

The points, however, that I want to focus on are: whether you are a male or female, be aware of using expensive, in-demand technology when walking alone. I know that is not always easy to do, but if you accept that someone wants to steal your iPhone then you may be a bit more cautious about your surroundings rather than being in Condition White and totally engrossed in your texting.

I can tell you that with my twenty-five-plus years of self defence training and knowledge I would not want to fight a kick-boxer. Yet a kickboxing instructor managed to be overwhelmed by two people and lost her items. I was not there and so do not know how it really panned out, but I am guessing that she struggled with them and did not punch or kick them or subject them to any serious violence. The point I want to make is that with all her training she clearly hadn't thought about fighting outside the ring, and had not given thought to actual self defence. I cannot stress enough: there is a huge difference between martial arts and combatives/self defence. I will comment on this a little further towards the end of this book.

***

This is a short story about someone I know who was involved in an attempted extortion or mugging in a busy part of Central London about a year ago. It demonstrates the kind of crimes that criminals are prepared to engage in, even in a highly policed area of London.

Jane was focussing on parking her car. A man appeared at the side of the car and tapped on the window. He was Caucasian (Eastern European), medium build, 5'10, casually dressed in jeans and leather jacket. Jane asked what he wanted and he showed her a gold ring in his hand. She waved him away and said it wasn't hers. He walked away and then returned whilst she was still parking. She opened her window and spoke to him. He said he had found a ring and thought it was hers. She said it wasn't but he insisted she take it. She took it and told him she was going to hand it in at a Police station. The man walked away a short distance whilst she continued to park. He then returned and knocked on her window, and asked her for some money, for food. She replied that she did not have any and if he wanted money he should get a job like everyone one else. He then asked for the ring back to which Jane replied she was going to take it to the Police station. He became abusive and kicked the car. Jane had finished parking and got out of the car. The man grabbed her arm. She struck his arm with her free hand, knocking it away from her. She then hit him in the face with a palm strike. Jane has had previous training in self defence (but many years ago).

The man fell to the ground due to the blow and she shouted at him that if he did not go away she will call the police. She threw the ring at him and he got up and ran off.

I asked her why she got out of the car. She replied that Central London has lots of people and she felt comforted by that.

My comments are these:

Do not feel the need to open your window. You can hear perfectly well with the window closed. If you must open it, only open it a few centimetres. Think that someone might try and put a knife in to threaten you, spray you with a substance or throw a rat through the window to get you to jump out. It goes without saying that your doors should always be locked.

Be suspicious of people approaching you. A small amount of paranoia is no bad thing.

Maintain distance/barriers. Understand that criminals will try and distract you by using aggression or simple plausible stories, or in this case, both.

Think before you act. Why would a man approach you and give you a ring (or any object of perceived value)? In this case the man used the pretence of "Is this your ring?" Jane knew it was not hers because she had not yet exited the car, so there was no need to engage the man in further conversation.

Once the man made his intentions apparent it was no longer safe to get out of the car. Call the Police. Call someone. Drive away if need be. Sit there with your hand on the horn. Do not expect a passer-by to help you. Most people will not get involved. As I mentioned earlier, they only see a snapshot of what is happening and will not understand the situation – and even if they did, most people would just walk on by. Jane in fact was going to a meeting nearby and the person she was meeting called her whilst the incident was in progress. He asked if she needed assistance. She said no. Never say no to an offer of assistance from a trusted individual! The man came anyway because he could hear that there was something amiss, although the incident was over by the time he got there.

Jane was lucky that the man did not physically attack her. He grabbed her arm which she managed to deal with then palm-struck him in the face, causing him shock and pain. Not everyone would have reacted as Jane did, in such a decisive manner. If you are grabbed and you manage to release yourself, get back in to your car or other immediate secure refuge. The attacker could have pulled a knife. Criminals routinely carry them and people from certain countries are much more likely to use them without fear of consequence.

He could also have had an accomplice that Jane was unaware of; in fact he most probably did. Understand that once you start to engage with someone who is clearly up to no good they may do everything they can to maintain control of the situation. If you are not strong-willed you could find yourself in a rapidly deteriorating situation that could end in (sexual) assault, stabbing, car theft, aggravated robbery or even abduction.

Security in your Vehicle

When we are travelling by car the key crimes we might be faced with are robbery of valuables, theft of the car, abduction or kidnapping of you or a passenger, and of course, random gratuitous violence.

In this section we discuss tactics for keeping safe when you are in your car, parking, returning to your car, as well as some other related matters.

When Driving

Whilst you are in your car, stationary, you are more susceptible to being attacked than when you are actually moving. From the moment you get into your car you should lock the doors. This should be an automatic action regardless of where you are. Most modern cars will automatically lock the doors when you drive over 5mph, but do not wait for that. I say that because when you get into your car in the street, or a car park, or anywhere, that is when you are most vulnerable. Locking the door will buy you valuable seconds should someone try to attack you or gain entry to the car.

Always wear your seat belt. Yes, it prevents you from going through the windscreen in an accident but just as importantly, it holds you in place if you have to take evasive action whilst driving. You cannot control a car when you are bouncing around inside and your distance from the steering wheel, accelerator, and brake pedal is forever changing.

When training people overseas in countries where civilians routinely carry firearms we used to

69

suggest not putting the seatbelt on until you had driven away from your parked up location in case you needed to shoot. But on reflection, especially as a civilian, if attacked, you are usually better off using the vehicle to escape the situation. So put your seatbelt on.

When stopped in traffic, always keep manoeuvrable distance between you and the vehicle in front. You should always try to leave enough space so that you can see the tarmac on the road in front of you; and if not the tarmac then at least the rear wheels of the vehicle in front. If you cannot see either then you are too close and it means that should you need to use your vehicle to extricate yourself from an attack at that time, you will not have the space to drive around the car in front.

Of course, you can always reverse to create space in front of you, but that will delay your escape. Imagine someone trying to get into your car to grab your handbag, or to grab you. You want to be able to just drive away, not waste valuable seconds reversing and then driving forwards giving them time to smash through the glass or threaten you with a weapon.

It is also possible that you have been hemmed in by the car behind you, intentionally or not. In this situation, you can shunt the cars in front and behind to create space, and then drive off. Clearly if one of the vehicles is a truck, bus, or a JCB then this will not be an option. If you do ever have to shunt, or realise you are going to have a low speed impact, keep your thumbs either off the steering wheel, or on the outer edge. A conventional steering-wheel hand grip will most likely break your thumbs on impact.

Bear in mind that you can also use the pavement or sidewalk if you are hemmed in and cannot drive around the ambush. You do not need to have an SUV or 4x4 to mount a curb; any car will do it, you just need to try and approach from a 30 degree angle so that you do not drive straight into the curb. You may cause some damage to the tyre or wheel, but most probably not, and that will be the least of your concerns at that moment.

A wealthy woman in Central America had such a situation some years back. Driving through an upmarket suburb on a dual lane avenue with a wide park-style central reservation running down the middle, she was ambushed by two vehicles, one in front and one behind. She wasn't immediately aware of the ambush but the car in front slowed and stopped. She braked hard and came to a stop just behind it, with not much manoeuvrable space. The car behind stopped close and men armed with pistols jumped out to kidnap her. The woman maintained her composure and drove backwards and forwards, creating a space by shunting the cars out the way, and drove around the front car.

The only mistake she made was after she drove a little way down the avenue she turned around and came back the other way on the other side of the central reservation, driving straight back past the kidnappers. She was lucky that they did not open fire. Admittedly, hitting a moving target at that range is very hard with handguns (it is easier with automatic assault rifles) but nevertheless she could still have been hit. It was an unnecessary risk to take but thankfully she escaped unharmed.

You might wonder why kidnappers would kill their intended victim during a failed kidnap attempt. The answer in Guatemala, where this incident occurred, was sheer stupidity. Kidnappers would often spend months planning a kidnap, but when it went wrong, they would kill the victim "by mistake" by being overzealous. The hoodlums employed by the kidnappers were generally not very intelligent.

***

When stopped in traffic, as well as maintaining distance between you and the car in front, always keep the vehicle in first gear on a manual car, or "drive" on an automatic. Never have the handbrake on unless you really need to use it.

When stationary in traffic jams, at lights, or at junctions, use that opportunity to remember to check your mirror to see what car is behind you and who is in it. If there are vehicles to your left or right make the effort to see what make or model vehicles they are, how many occupants are in them, and without making hard eye contact, have a look at their appearance. This can all be done with a single nonchalant glance. The idea is not to make anyone feel like you are paying them any particular attention; it should all be smooth and casual.

When parked up and waiting for someone, try to already be facing the direction you want to go, or more importantly, be waiting on the side of the road that will be easier for you to drive off quickly from. As when in traffic, try to park in a place with space in front of you so that you can drive off quickly. If there is a car in front of you and you cannot reverse back to give yourself space then have your wheels pointed outwards ready to move off.

You might think that some of these tips are so minor as not to be significant but I can assure you that if you are ever attacked you want to be able to escape with the minimum interference of things around you, and with maximum speed.

Use your mirrors effectively; all three of them. Have them positioned so that at a glance you can see the approaches to your vehicle from 360 degrees - the rear 180 degrees with your mirrors, the front 180 degrees just by scanning normally. Be aware of people approaching you, or who are in the road. For example, in many countries there are people who sell flowers by the roadside, or who start cleaning your windscreen for you, generally without permission, at traffic lights. Be wary of them. Try not to let them approach – mouth "no", shake your head or dismiss them with a wave of your hand. You can also consider sounding your horn.

If someone approaches your car when parked up, you should automatically be suspicious – things like that do not happen very often. As with the notes in the *Arms-Length Principle* section, try to ensure that you can see their hands. Do not be afraid of telling someone to step back away from the car to give you some distance. Understand that someone could be asking you for directions as a distraction and be vigilant against people approaching from other angles. Don't forget, if you do not like the look of someone, you can simply drive away. Do not feel obligated to stay and talk. Also, do not open your window. Or if you do, only open it a fraction, not enough for someone to get their hands inside. I repeat, keep an eye on their hands and make sure they are not carrying any spray or type of weapon.

We have already said to keep your doors locked. You should also keep your windows up where possible. Not so much when driving on an open road, but in slow moving traffic and stopped traffic. If you are driving a convertible, get rid of it. Just kidding, but understand that with the roof down you are very, very exposed.

A common tactic for stealing cars in some countries is to throw a rat or some small animal into the car. You rush out in a panic and the car gets stolen. Another similar method is for someone to lean in and grab your ear with a pair of pliers. You are unlikely to want to drive off in that situation! Having your windows closed or the roof up makes these tactics difficult for the would-be attackers to pull off.

There are numerous ways to get people out of their vehicles. Another is for the thieves or kidnappers to hang a length of fishing line from a bridge with a small but heavy object at the end of it. You drive along not seeing the fishing line or the weighted object. It hits your windscreen, cracks it and you pull over unaware that it was a ploy to get you to stop at that particular spot and that there are assailants waiting to ambush you. In such circumstances always carefully scan the area and consider driving on for a bit further to where it might be safer to pull over.

Another ploy for getting you out of the car, either to steal it or kidnap you, is to rear-end you. A car will drive into you from the rear, not too hard, just enough to give you a jolt. The idea being that you will immediately think it was an accident and just jump out your car, either in anger or concern. To avoid falling for this trick, never get out the car until you are sure it is legitimate.

Firstly, if there was no sound of skidding or braking prior to the impact then that would be a suspicious sign; it is common for people to notice at the last second that they are going to crash and slam on the brakes. Use your mirrors; who is in the car? Is it a little old man or lady, or two or three suspicious looking characters? Look around you as well, to see if anyone looks out of place, possibly working with the occupants of the car. If you are suspicious, drive forward a short distance and then pull over. Now you have distance in which to react, so observe patiently. If the occupants who caused the accident approach you, monitor them carefully. Be prepared to drive away if you are the least bit concerned. Note that it is an offence in most countries to leave the scene of an accident so you should call the police and report the incident as soon as possible. Only get out of your car if you feel it is safe to do so.

Currently there is an insurance fraud trend operating in many countries around the world whereby criminals fake accidents in order to claim on your insurance. For example, you may be waiting to make a turn and a car driving towards you slows down and the driver gestures for you to cross in front of them. They then roll or crash into you and deny that they signalled permission for you to make your turn. Although that does not relate to violence against you, understand that similar tactics could be used in an ambush situation (for car-jacking, robbery or abduction).

When arriving at your destination, be in Condition Yellow. You should already be in that state but if you are not, arrival times should be a trigger to switch back on and ramp up the awareness. Arriving and departing your primary and secondary locations (home, office, regular places you visit like dropping kids at school, gym) is when you are most vulnerable to a planned attack. I will explain this in more detail in the *Kidnapping* section. Whether you are a potential target for a kidnapping or just a random victim, scan the area around you; check for people looking out of place, for vehicles with occupants; anything that may not belong. If you do see something you are not happy with then just drive on by. You can always do a circuit, or pull up nearby and observe.

A method to help you be more aware as you approach your primary locations is to set a virtual demarcation zone about one kilometre around those places. As you approach the demarcation point, know to lower or turn off your car radio and to terminate any conversation you may be having either on your phone or with people in the car. You now have more resources available to you to scan the area, paying attention to the vehicles and people around you, to make sure that there is nothing different or suspicious that attracts your attention.

If you are attacked and manage to drive away, do not be concerned about breaking the law in order to escape. If you need to speed, then speed. If you need to jump a set of lights, and it is safe to do so, then do it. Do not be reckless and try not to drive in a panicked state, but do not worry about minor legal issues. In such situations your wellbeing is far more important than traffic law, and in these types of mitigating circumstances the police are highly unlikely to seek prosecution.

When Parking

You are especially vulnerable when approaching or leaving your car. This could be because you have parked in a place that is part of your routine (at or near your home or office) and someone is waiting specifically for you. It could be because you were in Condition White when parking randomly and did not see the danger signs of the suspicious people lurking nearby. Or it could be because you are returning to your car after shopping and are in a rush, carrying heavy bags, and not paying attention to the potential dangers around you.

Always give some consideration to where you park your car. Is it a safe place? Is it illuminated? Are there CCTV cameras? If there are lights and CCTV, try and park in a brightly lit area and in view of a camera. Criminals generally do not want to be seen. I will concede that generally CCTV does not stop crime; after all, people just put on baseball caps or hoodies to cover their faces. However, some people are concerned about being caught on CCTV.

Let us also not forget that we are trying to implement many small risk reduction strategies that, when combined, can help keep you safe.

If there is someone less aware than you, parked in a darker place that is not in view of a camera, then they are more likely to be attacked than you. Furthermore, in many town centres and shopping malls nowadays there is often operator-controlled CCTV. So apart from being safer in general, if you are in trouble, a response may be that much quicker.

Try to park in manned car parks, where there is an attendant, or where there is security. In London, for example, car parks are rated for their security, or at least the ones that have good security are noted. If you are planning where to park on your day out, choose one that you know is more secure.

Park as close as you can to the entrance of the shops as possible. If someone was following you from inside to out then they will quickly see that there are too many people around, and you can get back to safety quicker than had you parked in a corner on an upper level somewhere (if in a multi-storey car park).

Always reverse into a space. As said earlier, you should always try and leave your car facing the direction you want to go. In addition, it is easier to negotiate yourself into a narrow space between two cars rather than trying to drive in forwards.

Try to ensure that there is no sand, oil or lots of loose grit under your wheels. Maybe a car had a leak and sand was put down to absorb it. You do not want to park on a surface that could make your wheels spin when trying to drive off quickly.

After parking, before you switch off your engine give a final scan around the immediate area. It only takes a second and will keep you that much safer. Obviously, if there is something that causes you concern, do not get out of your vehicle and be ready to drive away. You can always come back another time.

Once you have left the safety of your car, do not loiter around the car park. Maybe someone phoned you, or you need to send a text message, or you are checking Facebook or someone WhatsApp'd you. Do not get engrossed in such things until you are in the store, unless you are in a secure and public place.

Don't leave signs in the car that a woman is driving. This could be a pair of driving shoes, coloured tissues, make up or anything predominantly feminine. It is said that certain predators will prey on particular types of women based on their personality make up, which can be discerned by such items.

At night, try not to use the internal compartment lights to rifle through your handbag or put make-up on. You can be seen for quite a distance without you being able to see who is watching. Don't be a goldfish in a goldfish bowl. All these tips apply to men too, although it is likely that fewer of you will be carrying handbags and wearing make-up.

As I have said in other parts of this book, you may be thinking that in your relatively safe, sane and normal Western country that going to your local "Westfield" style shopping mall has no more danger than sitting in Starbucks with your skinny cappuccino and carrot cake, and for the most part you might be right.

However crime can happen anywhere and it takes no extra time to practice the principles I have outlined above. And if you live in a country that faces violent crime on a daily basis, in places such as South Africa, or Central America or Mexico or Brazil, believe me when I tell you that these skills will become an intrinsic part of your daily life. If you do not live in those places, hopefully you will have an opportunity to visit them one day, and you will be able to conduct yourself in a manner that will keep you aware and safe.

Returning to your Car

If you can see your car from the safety of the store or entrance to the shopping mall then pause there and check the route to your car, and the area around it.

If there are suspicious people around then either wait and observe, go back inside and have a coffee, tell security to investigate, or even leave by another exit and take a taxi home. You can always get a lift back later from a friend.

Be super aware when you approach your car. Try and approach from an angle to see if anyone is hiding between the parked cars. Have a glance inside to make sure no one has gained entry and is waiting for you. Always try to have one hand free if possible, to defend or attack with, rather than both hands being burdened with bags. Being weighted down with bags also makes you appear more vulnerable.

Always have your remote and keys ready in your hand. This is to expedite entry to your vehicle, but keys can also be used as a weapon - if someone grabs you in any way you can rake the keys across their face or poke a larger key into their cheeks, eyes, neck or throat.

If you are loading bags or children into your vehicle, again, be aware during that period if anyone is approaching, especially if you are bent down and have a restricted view. Be as expeditious as possible.

Scan the area again just before you get into the car. If someone suspicious is approaching then you need to make a decision whether you have time to get into your car or whether you should go back to the potential safety of where you just came from.

When you get into your car lock the doors immediately, put the key in the ignition and start the engine. Consider releasing the handbrake, putting your foot on the footbrake and the car into gear, and only then do whatever your pre-drive rituals are (seatbelt, switching on your radio, placing your phone into a holder, getting out the satnav).

If someone does try to gain entry to your car before you are ready to start your journey, because you parked facing forwards you can calmly drive away.

A client of ours was kidnapped once. Well, he became a client after he was kidnapped. He came to us with his extended family to do a kidnap prevention course. That course contained almost everything you are reading in this book. When we asked him how he was kidnapped, this was his story: "I came out of my house in the morning and got into my car. I suddenly noticed a person standing on either side of my car, with guns. They appeared out of nowhere. I then did exactly what they told me to do."

I am commenting about this story at this juncture because I want you to understand that in almost all circumstances, if you are in your car when someone tries to gain entry or threaten you with a weapon, you need to put distance between you and them as quickly as possible.

You might be thinking that the attacker might shoot. That is possible. It is also unlikely because as said before, the attacker usually wants to use surprise to his advantage; he does not really want to hurt you, at least not in public. If he was there to kill you outright he would probably have shot already.

If he is standing there with a gun and says "I am going to count to three and then kill you" then you have no reason to wait around. He will shoot anyway so better to have distance between you. The further away you are from the gun the less accurate the shot will be, and hitting a moving target is a very hard thing to do indeed. Especially for people who are very unlikely to have spent much time on a shooting range under professional tutelage.

But above and beyond all of the above, if someone is trying to control you with a weapon you have to think why. If it is an abduction, what is the reason? Is it to inflict harm upon you somewhere more discreet? Is it to rape you? Is it to kill you? You read earlier that you must never allow yourself to be relocated anywhere. It cannot be for any good possible purpose. You need to take your chances where you are unless you are completely compromised.

Reverting back to the short kidnap account above, obviously the victim was in Condition White when he left his home and entered his car. I am pretty sure that the technology to beam down people so that they "suddenly appear from nowhere" doesn't exist (sorry to any science fiction fans out there). They were there; the client just did not see them. He should have looked from his windows in his house before leaving; from the peephole in his door before opening the door. After stepping outside he should have scanned the area before closing the door. Upon walking to his car he should have scanned the street and the area around his car. After getting in to his car he should have locked the doors, started the engine, and then scanned the area again.

He would have been able to drive away and escape if he had looked. Yes, as mentioned above, they could have shot at him. And in countries like Guatemala that is a very distinct possibility. However, with an estimated 50% of kidnap victims being killed after being kidnapped, it would have been better to take his chances. Thankfully he was released after a ransom was paid but he never did tell us what they did to him.

We will talk more about this in the *Kidnap Prevention* section later on.

If your proactive security fails and someone gains the opportunity to jump into the car with you, most likely you will not be able to discern whether it is a car thief, a rapist, or a murderer. Even if the intruder quickly says to you "Don't worry, I just need you to drive me away from this area" or "Don't worry, I won't harm you, I need to steal your car and I will drop you off down the road", do not believe him. In fact, you should already no longer be in the vehicle!

As soon as someone gets in to your car you must get out and move away quickly to a safe refuge. I know I have said it before but I will say it again: do not ever let someone take you to another location regardless of what excuse or subterfuge he or she employs.

You may have noticed that this is the first time I have referred to an attacker in the feminine. I decided to use the masculine as a "one size fits all" for convenience however the point needs to be raised that an attacker can be a woman just as easily as a man. And in the situation outlined above, a woman jumping in to your car is just as dangerous.

Women are perceived by both sexes as less threatening. If you are walking at night and hear footsteps behind you, if you see it is a woman then you automatically relax because she is unlikely to be a rapist, or murderer or psychotic killer. However, women can be violent sociopathic criminals just as much as men, or they can be utilised, by their own free will or under duress, or for money or drugs, as a lure, to cause you pause, to allay your fears, to get you to a vulnerable location or compromised position where the male accomplice(s) take over.

So, if a woman or possibly a teenager jumps into your car crying rape or seeking assistance, be extremely suspicious and unless there is immediate and apparent evidence to support their pleas for help, get out of there with extreme urgency and get to safety.

If you are being attacked in your car, try to have an improvised weapon to hand. In the UK it is illegal to carry pepper spray or any similar self-defence device. However, you can of course have with you an aerosol such as hairspray or deodorant that you can spray into the eyes and face of an assailant. It might be an idea to carry such an item in an easily accessible place in your car.

In other countries where it is legal to carry self-defence items, you should buy the strongest product on the market, just make sure you do not keep it beyond its shelf life otherwise it will not work when you need it most! Be aware that when it comes to pepper sprays and the such like that some spray a mist and some spray a liquid, and depending which way the wind is blowing (if you use it outside) that you may well get some of it on you. Equally, using it in a confined space such as your car or an enclosed room will often mean that you will breathe some in or get some in your eyes, but less so hopefully than your attacker!

When it comes to carrying and using weapons make sure you have trained with them and are fully prepared and committed to using them. Otherwise your attacker will just take it away from you and use it against you.

If someone does somehow jump into your passenger seat and for whatever reason you do not have the time or opportunity to get out straight away, and for situations whereby the unwelcome guest has a weapon, you can consider accelerating forwards briefly and then slamming on the brakes as hard as you can. Obviously you should be wearing your seatbelt and hopefully at this stage they had yet to put theirs on. At relatively low speeds they will have a shock and get thrown forwards. At higher speed there will be more damage to them as they will probably hit the windscreen. Once you have stopped, remove your seatbelt and escape the vehicle and seek help.

If someone opens a rear door and gets into the back seat and tries to threaten and control you from there you can do the same acceleration tactic. However, be aware that if the attacker is immediately behind you, depending on the height of your seat compared to theirs, and whether you have your headrest up, that when they fly forwards you may be struck by their head which could prove fatal to you or cause whiplash. Be aware of the same situation if you have a front seat passenger and the assailant is sitting behind them. In such circumstances it will depend on the level of threat as to whether you try such a manoeuvre or not; perhaps limit the speed that you try it at.

In extreme circumstances, an alternative to accelerating and braking when an attacker is sitting next to you is to accelerate briefly in order to crash into the car in front, or a parked car, or a lamppost or curb. This might sound extreme but if you are being abducted then the measure is within proportion. Keep the speed below 30mph. Understand that your airbags will most likely deploy (depending on the speed and where the impact is). Keep your body pushed back into your seat as far away from the steering wheel as possible, and keep your thumbs off the wheel as previously mentioned. This is so you are less affected by the exploding airbag and also by the impact of the crash. Be ready to release your seatbelt, get out of the car and make your escape, leaving a disorientated and potentially hurt attacker.

Hopefully however, if you maintain your awareness and keep your doors locked and your windows closed you will reduce the likelihood of ever having to be in any of these situations.

Route Planning

Always give some thought about where you are going before you leave a safe area. Think about the route you want to take; will it be particularly congested at that time of day; will you be driving through a rough neighbourhood?

Plan your route and have some knowledge of the surrounding areas. Do not make rash decisions and take unknown turn-offs that could lead to dead ends or dangerous places.

Think about potential danger spots or choke points on the route. By this we mean places that could inhibit you from escaping a situation quickly such as one way streets, narrow roads or bottle necks; or locations that could be used to the advantage of an attacker against you.

Do not hesitate to take a longer route if it means a safer journey.

We already mentioned *Safe Havens* in the *Security in the Street* section. They are just as important when driving. If you are being followed, or chased, you need to know where to go.

As said, options can be (but not limited to) embassies, certain shopping malls, universities, international hotels, hospitals, police stations and military bases; anywhere where there is a good level of reliable and effective security.

It goes without saying that you should have a fully charged mobile phone with you at all times.

Where possible always notify someone that you are on your way to wherever you are going, including stops on the way and the route you are intending to take. That way, if you do not arrive by a certain time they will know to be concerned and can contact the authorities if they cannot get hold of you.

Anti-Ambush Driving

If you are living in a country that is rife with crime, where you drive from your gated residential compound to your secure office building or the secure shopping mall because it is too dangerous to walk; where you are faced with the real risk of violent crime on a daily basis with car-jackings, abductions and kidnappings featuring frequently in the news, then you might consider taking an evasive driving course.

In countries like the UK these types of courses are rare but they exist; they are just something you do not hear about because most people are not concerned with such levels of violent crime. But if you live in a crime-ridden country, are travelling to one, or being stationed in one by your company, then you should seriously consider enrolling in such a course. If you are a wealthy person, a celebrity, a business executive or anyone that could be at risk of attack or kidnap, you should learn how to drive defensively.

It is a fact that the majority of kidnappings and assassinations are vehicle based, and driving is a major part of most people's routines! Learning how to control your vehicle in an attack situation will prepare you mentally and physically for escaping the situation.

When we were working in Central America in the nineties we were the local representatives of the most renowned defensive driving school in the world, which was based in the United States. We ran a fair few courses and although it is a serious topic and skill, they were a lot of fun to teach.

Unfortunately, just as it is not feasible to teach you how to fight in words, it isn't really possible to teach you defensive driving techniques in a book.

The one piece of advice I can give you however is this: if you are in your car and are attacked, never get out and never stop driving unless you have crashed or are facing an insurmountable ambush. An attacker moving towards you with a weapon is not an ambush you cannot get away from. You can accelerate and run him over. You can do a handbrake turn to reverse direction without stopping. You may even have the room to just turn using normal driving techniques. There is the option of doing regular Y turns, or a reverse one-eighty (J-turn). If you already had speed it is also an option to drive around the attacker although, as mentioned previously, you will be more susceptible to gunfire as you pass him by. In most cases this should be a last resort only.

Having a several-ton industrial mechanical digger or a bus blocking your path will probably be problematic as is having your engine totalled. But if your car is drivable then understand that you want to maintain motion at all times and drive around or through the attack. Never stop or give up.

The majority of people can only control up to about 40% of their cars' capabilities. I would even dare say that most people can only control their car to 40% of their own capabilities. Driving day to day on normal roads with comfortable bends means that no one uses their vehicle to anywhere near its potential.

On a professional one-day evasive driving course you will learn how to control your car to up to 90% of your capabilities, and learn how your car handles when driven evasively.

Understand also that evasive driving courses are not just for people under active threat. After reading this book and understanding "everyday" situations that you may be faced with, knowing how to drive your car better will give you much more confidence to escape a situation. Also, the same course will help you control your car better when faced with an emergency accident situation whilst driving; you will have a much better chance of avoiding a collision.

If you do enrol in a course, make sure they include some pressure testing drills once they have taught you the driving techniques. The driving will be demanding, and at times adrenalin-fuelled, but pressure testing those drills in simulated attack or ambush situations is essential. Just like we have learned to keep distance between ourselves and perceived threats, if you are attacked you must create distance between you and the attackers, and escape the "kill-zone".

Finally, make sure your car is maintained adequately. Check the oil and water, and make sure your tyres and brakes are in good order. Most people keep their tyres pumped to a minimum. The maximum PSI for every tyre is written on the sidewall of the tyre. Keep them pumped to the car vehicle manufacturer's recommended level. If your tyre is severely under inflated and you conduct an evasive manoeuvre the tyre can actually come off the wheel. Also, a poorly inflated tyre is more susceptible to punctures, results in lower fuel economy, and wears faster.

Security in the Home

An Israeli in El Salvador once said to me "Everyone needs their own little corner of the world where they can feel safe and comfortable".

You should make your home as secure as reasonably possible; you spend at least half your life there. This is especially so if you own the property, as the investment in security will be long term.

When someone moves to a new home they usually feel quite insecure. They notice the access points, the lack of security and whatever the various vulnerabilities are. However, after a couple of weeks they have become accustomed to the property, know the creaks and noises that it makes at night, and suddenly they feel secure. Have they enhanced the security at all though? No they have not. Are they any more secure than the day they moved in? No they are not. This is almost like the 7 seconds to escape in a kidnap situation – because they did not act on their concerns early on, they have now justified why they do not need to spend any money. This is a mistake in my opinion.

Home security can be split between physical and electronic protection. Before spending money on lighting, intruder alarms or CCTV, your best investment is in making physical enhancements to prevent someone from gaining entry. Your primary concern is to protect yourself and your loved ones from attack, and then of course your valuables.

If we follow the main self-protection theme of this book, an intruder could be breaking in to your home to cause you physical harm such as rape, physical assault or murder. Obviously it is far more common that they are breaking in to steal, expecting no one to be home, or thinking you are fast asleep.

Home invasions (i.e. when you are in the home at the time of the break in) are quite rare in most countries. Even in extremely violent places such as Guatemala City, criminals rarely break into homes when the residents are there because they might get shot. Strangely, in Johannesburg for example, the chances of getting shot by a resident are significantly higher, yet bizarrely there are far more home invasions.

This chapter will help you to understand what measures you can take to protect your home, whether against an intruder trying to do you harm or an intruder breaking in for simple theft purposes.

Doors and Windows

There are three main ways someone will open an external door to your home: force, such as in kicking or shouldering; picking or breaking the lock; or jimmying the frame.

Doors should have strong locks fitted correctly. If you can replace your front door with a solid wooden one, or have a strong metal door and frame fitted with multipoint locking then that is great. There are lots of manufacturers of high end security doors – some admittedly are very expensive and the cost will depend on your level of risk and whether you can afford it.

Locks should also extend into the hinge side. For wooden doors you can fit hinge bolts which just drill in to the door side and slot into the frame when the door is closed. These should be fitted especially on doors that are hinged externally as hinges can easily be removed to gain access. If you do not have a metal door with a metal frame then you should consider reinforcing the frame with metal bars, which are readily available.

If you have a wooden door with a type of mortise lock fitted into it the door is susceptible to shattering around the lock when kinetic force is applied (someone kicking or shouldering it).

However, special mortise reinforcement plates can be mounted on either side of the door with the lock in between them which will prevent this from happening.

All the previous recommendations will make it almost impossible for your door to be kicked in. Also if the door fits the frame correctly, and the locks are fitted professionally and close into the frame properly, then jimmying open a door will be very difficult. Of course, understand that there are ways to bypass most security but bypassing security takes a lot of time, effort, and having the correct tools to hand. This creates exposure to the person breaking in and makes it far less likely to happen, unless you are a high risk location or person.

Picking locks is incredibly rare in burglary situations. It is far easier to learn about the lock and break it or drill it depending on the type of lock.

However these sorts of incidents are also quite rare as there are usually easier ways to gain entry.

Windows are problematic. Always fit strong insurance-approved window locks where possible. Some types of windows have integrated locks or even multipoint locking. But obviously glass can be broken and access can be gained without opening the actual frame. You can consider putting protective film on the windows which will make them difficult or impossible to break. Of course if you have the types of window that are externally beaded then understand that the glass can be removed with little difficulty. Thieves have also been known to remove entire window frames together with the glass. But again, this requires time and opportunity.

Of course, collapsible gates or security grilles or bars can be fitted internally. This is a good idea, especially for particularly vulnerable windows (e.g. those that are accessible by low roofs in secluded locations). We do not usually recommend security bars to be fitted externally because then criminals have direct access to them and can use various means to remove them. External bars may also provide the opportunity for an intruder to climb up them giving access to a first or second floor window or balcony.

Electronic security shutters are also available. These can be fitted internally or externally but if they are fitted externally ensure they have insurance-rated locking mechanisms that are not easily forced, or that there is some sort of alert that can be triggered if they are forced.

If you have sturdy drain pipes running up from the ground to windows or balconies higher up then you can use anti-climb paint to make it difficult for someone to climb up. Alternatively, or in conjunction with anti-climb paint, you can get a spiked collar fitted that will make it very awkward to climb past.

You should walk around your house from the outside and see how, with basic tools, you would gain entry. Can you do it with ease? Will you be seen by members of the public or neighbours? Will it take too long or be too difficult? Will it make too much noise? Is there a skylight or upper floor access that can be reached by climbing on to your neighbour's roof, which might be easier to do? Or if you live in an apartment, is it easier to kick open your neighbour's door to gain access to your balcony?

Illumination

Some people are strong advocates of external lighting whilst others less so. Criminals do not want to be seen. Lighting will expose them. However, if the house sits behind a high wall or fence with no neighbours overlooking, then the light you have kindly provided may just provide illumination to aid your intruder in their break-in.

For most people, external illumination is more of a pro than a con. It is important to ensure the lights are maintained, that you check regularly that they work and that bulbs are replaced in a timely fashion if blown. If you find that a light is not working then you should also be aware that perhaps someone smashed the bulb to see how long it takes you to notice, or because they had planned to come back that night in the darkness for their intrusion.

Lighting can be left on in the dark, ideally using dusk-to-dawn timers so that they turn off by themselves as soon as day breaks. Having floodlights with integrated movement detectors is fine but they generally do not work that well — they can trigger quite a lot for no apparent reason or may not trigger when you expect them to. If you can afford it, it would be more ideal to fit the lights at the height you want, which may involve some strategic design, and have them connected to professional external movement detectors linked to a lighting control. That way, the system will provide more comprehensive and professional detection and you would have been able to choose whatever type of light you wanted.

If you do connect to a lighting panel then you can programme an alert that will beep at night so that you can be informed if the lights are triggered. Obviously if you have "wild" animals strolling around your perimeter at night you do still risk some false activations.

While we are on the topic of lighting, be aware that if you are at home and you do not have curtains or blinds drawn, especially at night, then anyone observing from the street or edge of your property will be able to see all your movements and locations, whilst you essentially cannot see out.

If you are away or will not be home for a few days, try to set up a lamp on a timer so that the light(s) come on for certain periods so that your home does not look empty. If you have a way for remotely controlling your TV then that too is a good option – there is nothing more convincing of someone being at home than the blue flicker of the TV in a darkened room.

Electronic Security

After making the physical security enhancements to your home you can now consider electronic security. This would normally be either an intruder alarm or CCTV camera system. If you had to choose between the two, then an intruder alarm is your best line of defence. Firstly, it is far cheaper than CCTV and secondly, an alarm will do far more for you to stop a crime than CCTV.

A professionally fitted intruder alarm looks... professional. Many burglars will automatically avoid breaking in to homes with a security system fitted. If you have a bell box outside that is ancient and rusty, or has no logo or company name on, then it will look just how it is: old and defunct or a DIY installation that most likely will not be communicating to anyone if activated.

Apart from the deterrent factor, if someone does break in, the alarm activating with sirens internally and externally will cause the intruder to feel very vulnerable and exposed. He will not know if the neighbours will come, or if the system is communicating to a response company or to the police, or other keyholders. If he does not run away immediately he will certainly limit the amount of time he spends inside.

You do hear the occasional horror story whereby an alarm activates, the police or security arrive, see no signs of a break in and leave without entering the property. When the owner or keyholder arrives and disarms the alarm he finds intruders patiently waiting for him inside. This is very rare but something to be aware of. Always exercise maximum caution when entering your property after an activation. Always conduct a good perimeter search first and ideally have someone with you.

As a rule of thumb, every ground floor room with external access should have detection devices in it. Upper floors are more discretionary and will depend on valuables, ease of access and a threat assessment of the risks against you.

Whereas in the past intruder alarms were mostly connected to the Police or to a response centre, nowadays many just ring locally at the property or have a dialler that notifies the homeowner or their keyholders of the activation. To be honest, anything is better than nothing. If your system does not communicate anywhere then hopefully the external strobe can be programmed to continue to flash after the siren has silenced, so that when you arrive home you at least have a visual alert to notify you that there has been an activation and that you should proceed with caution.

For higher-end properties or people at high risk, you can have dual-path signalling systems. Traditional signalling of alarms is via the standard telephone line. If that is cut by the intruders (very rare) or the line goes down due to a fault with the telephone company (less rare!) then there is a GSM or GPRS back up path that will notify you of primary path failure and also let you know if there are any subsequent activations.

Whether systems signal or not, I always recommend that you have a panic button fitted. The cost of a panic button connected to your alarm is a nominal amount in comparison to the main system, but the peace of mind is huge. I can cite an example of a home invasion in London whereby the very aggressive and intimidating intruders assaulted the husband in front of his wife, and then forced the wife upstairs to rape her.

As they entered the bedroom she ran over to the side of the bed where their panic button was fitted and pressed it. The alarm activated and the intruders thankfully fled immediately. That was a sickening and horrendous situation but goes to show that despite the gang of intruders having the confidence to force their way into the house, the wild aggression shown towards the husband, and the fact they were going to rape the wife, when confronted with being caught they did not calmly rape the wife. They did not go back and further attack the husband. They fled. They fled because ultimately they had lost control of the situation and they did not want to face the consequences.

***

CCTV is a great tool to have, but it is generally quite costly and it is still comparatively rare to find in homes. CCTV is unlikely to stop a crime, although just like the burglar that will not break into a house with an alarm system, there are criminals who will shy away from a house with

CCTV because they will see it as that much more of a harder target.

CCTV is good for trying to work out what happened before, during and after a criminal act; it can help in catching the criminal. However, the reason why CCTV does not usually stop crime from happening is because the perpetrator usually just needs to cover his head or face and then cannot be easily identified. However, if you have installed good quality equipment and are recording in "high-quality real-time" then a lot of information can be gleaned.

Furthermore, the design of the system is essential. It is common practise, and not a very good one, to just place a camera on each corner of the house that will give a general overview of the immediate area. Unfortunately, in that situation a person walking outside the house will look about an inch big on the viewing screen; this will not be useful for recognition or identification purposes. So, in addition to those overview cameras it is good practice to also fit some cameras lower down, or still high up but focussed on a specific "choke point", such as the gate or main entrance, where the intruder has to pass by, so that you have more chance of getting a clearer image of their face.

It is often said that a low quality camera system is better than no camera system, but is it really? Not if it will not ever provide you with useful images; possibly yes if it is more for the deterrent effect or for just giving you a basic view, i.e. is there someone there or isn't there. Understand that cheap CCTV systems are cheap for a reason. They usually do not have good processors or lenses and will provide low quality, grainy images in anything but the most perfect of weather conditions.

Unless you have good external lighting at night, fit cameras with integrated LEDs otherwise your system will be useless fifty percent of the time.

One proactive benefit of having a CCTV system is for checking the perimeter of your house before you leave, and potentially before you arrive home. Obviously, you can always use the peephole in your front door or look out the window but with CCTV you can see at a glance. Nowadays all Digital Video Recorders (DVRs) have web servers or smartphone apps and you can view your system remotely to check that the perimeter and approaches are clear (assuming you have coverage of those locations).

Another benefit is for when you are at home and hear a noise. Rather than go outside to investigate or open a door to a potential stranger you can view the cameras from inside the property. Obviously at the upper end of the scale you can have external perimeter detectors connected to your CCTV system that if triggered, will send images to a Video Receiving Centre. The centre can then remotely challenge the "intruder" or call a security patrol, the police or keyholders.

Dealing with Conmen and Intruders

Many people are robbed in their home after being conned into letting the thief inside. There are a lot of confident criminals out there who are happy to play a role to gain access. They could claim to be from a utility company such as telephone, electricity or gas, or they could be delivering a package as a courier, or could even pretend to be a policeman.

Never ever allow someone into your home that has turned up unexpectedly. Even if they were expected you must check their identification. If you are unsure about them, for example it is someone you haven't seen before, then you can always call the company to confirm that the person outside is indeed their company representative.

If someone has arrived unsolicited then that is cause for even further caution and suspicion. Never confirm their identity with a number that they have just provided you with. Always use a number you already know or that you look up yourself. It is very common for the criminal to give you a plausible looking ID or business card. You ring that number and someone answers in the company name but in reality that someone is sitting in the car down the road, or is the girlfriend or accomplice sitting at home somewhere.

Never feel obligated to let them in. Never fall for the excuse that they just need to check that one tiny thing that will take just a minute. Never let them come in and use your bathroom.

Remember, a professional conman will have the gift of the gab. He will have all the answers and will do what he can to coerce you into to letting him in. Normal people do not do that. Do not let yourself get pressured into allowing him inside.

You may be thinking that with all this discussion with them you are feeling vulnerable and self conscious, and if you are a timid person by nature that you may well capitulate and let them in. There is one easy solution for this which I have not yet mentioned. During all the above you should not have opened your front door. Always keep a physical barrier between you and them. If you have a door entry system then obviously you have no need to have opened the door at all. Ideally the handset should not be directly behind the front door. If you do not have a door entry system then you can simply go upstairs and talk down to them from a window. The height and distance from them will help you relax and allow you more confidence.

Understand also that many criminals work in pairs or teams. Whilst one is engaging you at the front door trying to sell you stuff you do not want their accomplice has gained entry through your open back door or window and is stealing your iPod, iPad, iPhone and MacBook Air as well as your family jewellery, credit cards and the cash you thought you had hidden well. Be wary of distractions!

All of the above was written using the example of someone trying to gain your confidence to let you inside for the purpose of theft. But think back to what I wrote about in the *Security in the Street* and the *Security in your Vehicle* sections, about how to never let a criminal relocate you to another place where you are secluded. Now think about what would happen to you if the conman was not a thief, but a rapist or a murderer and you are already in your secluded home. That knock on your door could be the culmination of weeks of stalking or hostile reconnaissance against you, or it could be the rapist or murderer who just followed you back from the park or store.

Also, remember what I said in the *How to be an Easy Victim* chapter at the very beginning of this book: a robber could become a rapist or even a murderer. Maybe the conman was a thief, but is unbalanced, or feeling sexually frustrated, and has gained entry to your home to steal from you. He sees that you are nervous and is emboldened by your compliance or submissiveness. He then takes advantage and commits a sexual assault against you, after which — if he panicked and was not thinking straight — could result in him trying to kill you to stop you talking. It might sound farfetched but unfortunately things like that happen.

I cannot stress enough: do not let people in to your home that you are unsure of. You might feel more comfortable talking to strangers whilst standing in the comfort and "security" of your home compared to how vulnerable you feel in the street at night in a rough neighbourhood, but you should treat unknown people with the same level of suspicion.

***

If someone breaks in to your home whilst you are there what should you do? Obviously this will be a very frightening situation, and is thankfully quite rare. But it does happen. Many people wake up in the morning to find that thieves had broken in during the early hours of the morning and cleared out their valuables and stolen their car. The thought of someone having been in your house whilst you were asleep is not a pleasant one.

But for situations that you are aware of, you need a course of action. Unfortunately as with most things in life there are myriad situations that each will have several potential solutions, so let us just look at a couple of viable options.

The first thing is to keep safe. Do not expose yourself to the intruder if you can help it. You may not know how many of them there are, what their intentions are, if they are carrying weapons, or whether they are drunk or on drugs. They may or may not be in full control of their mental faculties.

Lock yourself in the room you are in. If you have children or other vulnerable people in the house then try to get to them and then lock yourselves in a room. If you are near an exit then instead of locking yourselves in a room then perhaps leave the property. But as I said earlier in the book, do not just leave a place in a panic without knowing that you can get to a place of safety quickly. Maybe you can drive away or get to a neighbour.

If you lock yourself in a room try to make sure it is one that is not easily accessible from the outside by the intruders. That said, a way in for them is potentially a way out for you, so that should be a consideration if they are nowhere near that part of the property at that time.

Call the police, or press your panic button, or both depending on who responds to your panic button. If your elderly mother is your only keyholder and your alarm is programmed to call her then clearly you do not want her responding. Unless of course she carries a shotgun!

There is probably little benefit in hiding quietly, as eventually the thieves may come across you. And remember, they may not be thieves or even if they are they may be unbalanced or have secondary intentions.

If you can control lights in the house then turn them on. Again, it will make the intruders feel more vulnerable. You can make a lot of noise. We spoke about bluffing in the *Security in the Street* section. Shout out "Bill, Jimmy, get the weapons, there are people downstairs" and then make lots of stomping sounds. This is of course if you are in a house with more than one floor.

Understand that 99.9% of burglars do not want confrontations. So in the above situation, once the intruder knows they are not alone or that you are now aware of their presence, they may flee. In most cases they will.

Every country will have had cases highlighted in the news whereby a homeowner confronted an intruder. More often than not one or the other was severely wounded and in lots of cases one died. Either the home owner stabbed or shot the intruder or vice versa. It is better if you do not have a confrontation. However, sometimes it will be impossible to avoid and sometimes you will have the upper hand.

I joked before about the mother with the shotgun, but if you do have a shotgun or a pistol or any type of firearm then obviously this is the time to have it close by, and be prepared to use. You will know the law of your land regarding self defence and the use of weapons. There is nothing scarier for an intruder than to hear the sound of a gun cocking followed by a bellowed command to "Stay away!"

If you have a home with internal doors that can be locked it is a good idea to keep them locked when you retire for the night. This will slow down any intruder trying to make their way around your house.

I said earlier to turn on the lights. There are times for that but it is also an alternative, depending on the situation, to leave the lights off especially if it is very dark and the intruder does not know the layout of your home. You can position your furniture in a way to ensure there are no direct lines across any room to any door, which may help slow down an intruder if they break in and you are in that room. A couple of seconds can be the difference between life and death. In the dark, negotiating furniture for someone unfamiliar with the room or house layout is potentially difficult.

It goes without saying that you should be able to navigate around your own home in the darkness. Practice it, but be careful you do not knock yourself out! Think of the term "slow is smooth and smooth is fast". You can always speed up once more familiar.

Some homes may have a room that would make a good safe room. It could be an en-suite dressing room or bathroom, but should be a place with thick walls and no access from the outside. The door and frame should be reinforced, as should the walls and ceiling if they are simple plasterboard or similar. If you are an at-risk person or are wealthy then you should designate a safe room and get an appropriate door fitted. I mentioned earlier about the types of doors you can get. The finish on them is very professional and they are made to blend in to any decor. You can also get different levels of protection, against something simple like a hammer or an axe to fully armoured against firearms.

If you do make a safe room then ensure it is kitted out correctly and that as a minimum you have a dedicated land line and mobile phone, water, some food, a first aid kit (for wounds and any medication you might be on), torches, blankets for warmth and possibly oxygen and gas masks. You would hope that you would not need to stay in there for more than a few minutes. However, in the worst-case scenario, if there ended up being a hostage situation with the intruders holed up in your house whilst the police negotiate with them, then at least you have basic amenities to hand!

If you have an upstairs to your house and there is no easy access from the outside to the upper floors and a break-in is most likely to occur on the ground floor, then you can consider fitting a high security door either at the top or the bottom of the stairs to create a virtual "safe floor".

✳✳✳

It should go without saying that no tools should be left lying around externally. Garages, garden sheds and outhouses should all be secured. Ladders should be securely chained to a wall.

Intruders often use items they have found laying around in your garden as a means to gain entry. It saves them having to carry incriminating tools around with. Trust me when I tell you that it will make you feel far more upset when you find out that you contributed to your own intrusion.

If you have perimeter walls or garden fences, make them as sturdy and as high as you are permitted to. If you can have some sort of intruder spikes at the top, then fit them.

✳✳✳

Try to give the impression that your property has nothing worth stealing. Obviously in today's day and age most people have something worth stealing, but try not to do anything that causes your house to stand out from the crowd. That obviously is quite difficult to do if you have a very nice house and do not have hidden underground parking for the Ferrari. But on a smaller scale, do not leave the box of your brand new 60″ plasma outside for all to see.

Make it difficult for an intruder to know whether the house is occupied or not. Have sufficient visible security to make your house look like it will be too much trouble to break into. It is the same concept as you being a hard target in the street. Make your home a hard target. Another home in your street probably will not be as well protected.

Outside your Home

I mentioned in the *Security in the Vehicle* chapter about scanning the area of your destination as you arrive, and it is obviously equally as important, in fact more so, when you approach on foot. In a vehicle, if there are assailants waiting for you on foot then you are in a much better position to escape. On foot, you have less options and less security.

If you live in an affluent neighbourhood you may well have heard of street robberies in your area. I can give you many stories of people arriving, blissfully unaware of their surroundings, who are suddenly confronted by knife wielding robbers who politely relieve them of their "his and hers" matching Rolex watches and all their cash.

After getting this far in the book you should have enough awareness and understanding of tactics to see the above situation in advance, and take steps to avoid it. I have mentioned this in this section because it ties in with people waiting for you to return home in order to force you inside, possibly for you to disarm your intruder alarm, and then rob you and force you to open the safe or divulge the location of your valuable jewellery.

If you have an intruder alarm with a duress code facility that will either audibly or silently alert the authorities, then use it. If you have a panic button, press it. In theory, you do not want to enter your house with the intruder. If you can escape from them outside, scream for help, run to a neighbour, or stand in a busy road, then do so.

However, there may well be times when you are outnumbered and severely compromised, in which case you may not have the means or opportunity to escape. In such cases, you can only hope that you will not be hurt, and keep your options open to get to safety at your earliest possibly opportunity.

It can happen that as you arrive at home, either on foot or by car, you see people hiding in the shrubbery or bushes of your driveway. I know of an instance where this happened, and after stealing the woman's jewellery the robbers tried to abduct her by forcing her away from her property into a waiting vehicle. Thankfully she resisted and they gave up due to the time it was taking and the attention it was drawing. Undoubtedly they were abducting the woman for rape.

In the above situation, if you have arrived by car then you know what to do. Do not panic, but drive out and away as quickly as possible. This is where evasive driving courses come into their own; not just for the driving skills, but to be able to back out of your driveway with the fear and pressure of people banging on your windows and trying to open your doors.

Another tactic, a more elaborate one, is for the criminals to wait outside expensive restaurants or similar locations, choose a victim when they leave, and follow them back home. Alternatively, they lay in wait in a darkened secluded part of a street, at a choke point where they can observe the occupants of cars as they drive past, and when they have chosen their victim they follow them the short stretch of distance to the residence.

113

When the unaware couple pull up outside their house and get out they are overwhelmed and possibly overpowered by a fast aggressive assault that relieves them of their valuables and possibly their vehicle too. It has been known for this type of robbery to extend into the house.

We know by now to be in a heightened state of awareness when we are arriving and departing our home. In the above situation you only need to be marginally aware of your surroundings to notice the possible attack, and you can just continue driving whilst you call the police. We will cover this more in the *Kidnap Prevention* section.

Kidnap Prevention

Much of what we have learned from the previous chapters will be reinforced in this next section of the book. If you are sitting reading this in Melbourne, or Quebec City, or Vienna you might be wondering why on earth I have included a section on kidnap prevention. Most of you living in a modern country with professional and effective law enforcement will be wondering the same thing.

However, if I replace the word "kidnap" with "abduct" would you still be as perplexed? Whilst you may not be at risk of kidnap, which is usually for a ransom, you may, or someone you are responsible for, be abducted for other reasons such as robbery, rape or murder.

Also, one day you may travel to some of the most beautiful countries in the world, where unfortunately kidnapping could almost be the national pastime. Or, you might actually be living in one of those countries; amazing scenery, fantastic weather and great people, where kidnapping is rife.

No matter who you are, understanding this type of threat is advantageous and can only help protect you further. Many of the points I cover here complement the knowledge already gained from the earlier sections of this book and will help you keep yourself and your loved ones safe.

Also understand that although we are talking about kidnapping and abduction, the information on surveillance is also useful for people under threat of assassination.

The Kidnap Selection Process

Victims of kidnappings are usually not selected at random. Rather, the kidnappers will have a set of criteria to apply to their target selection process; a process designed to give them the optimum chance of success.

There are essentially four stages to the kidnap selection process. However, it is important to acknowledge that these stages may not happen in order, or at all, and that these stages could take place over several weeks or months, or in fact as quickly as several minutes or hours. This will make more sense as we progress into the chapter.

Professional kidnappers are usually very methodical in selecting their final targets. They do not want, and cannot afford, a failure. Organising a kidnapping takes huge resources and so the investment must justify the potential return. Also, kidnapping is a high-risk crime and getting caught is something the kidnappers will be doing their utmost to avoid. Therefore, they will generally be very diligent in their planning and only take calculated risks. That said, please understand that what might be a "viable risk" to a kidnapper will far surpass your perception of viable risk. What is likely to take you outside your comfort zone might be more usual for a criminal, especially if this is not their first forage into crime.

Stage 1

The first stage is usually to compile a list of potential targets. The kidnappers will scan the media to find perspective candidates. In most cases they will be looking for wealthy people or families. They could also consider employees of wealthy people or corporations. For example, they could kidnap an au pair working for a wealthy family who might then feel obligated to pay, or a valued (and maybe essential) employee working for a large corporation; perhaps the corporation will not want negative publicity if they are complicit in the demise of a member of staff.

A well-executed selection procedure will equate to a good group of potential candidates for the kidnappers to choose from. The targets are usually not chosen based on emotion or aggression, as in it should not be personal. That said, obviously there will be people chosen who are known to the kidnappers, and perhaps the whole kidnapping attempt was fuelled by an idea developed by someone who actually knows the victim, has a grudge, or thinks that person will be an easy target.

For example, an employee or ex-employee might have a wealthy boss about whom he knows all his or her movements; or a tradesperson who has worked in, or has access to a wealthy person's home. So it is possible that rather than there be a professional gang of kidnappers looking for a target, that there is already a target and someone has to create his "amateur" kidnap gang.

A kidnap can also be politically motivated. The kidnapper's maybe interested in what the victim represents. Or they could be a "green" group that has decided to kidnap an oil company executive because of the damage they are doing to the planet.

Regardless of motive, in most cases the kidnappers will be looking for financial profit. Yes, there could be other goals, but most likely it will be about earning money.

If you are someone who could be a potential target, know that there are probably dozens or hundreds of other potential targets that also fit the kidnappers' criteria. Just because you may make the shortlist does not mean that you will be chosen; the kidnappers will put you all through the selection process to find the easiest and most practical target.

This first stage deals mostly with the selection process a kidnap gang may go through when choosing a victim who is not yet known to them. This may not necessarily apply to you, although you never know! The next stages however are relevant to everyone.

Stage 2

The kidnappers have their list of potential targets. In this stage they will refine that list and reduce the number of potential targets by a process of elimination. They do this by starting to gather intelligence about the lifestyle and habits of the people on the list.

For you this is the most important phase of the process. This is because if you understand how the kidnappers will work to verify you as a potential target then you know what to do to avoid making the next shortlist! By using basic tactics, some of which you have already learned, you can develop a personal security programme that will ensure they see you as a hard target and dismiss you from their list.

The kidnappers will spend considerable time conducting initial surveillance on each potential target. The most important information they are looking for is your daily schedule. They will be looking for accurate details. What time do you leave home in the morning? What time do you arrive at work? Do you take the same route? Do you take your children to school? Do you stop off for a workout at the gym before or after work, and if so, which days?

They will look for a pattern. They will know your routine better than you and your family.

They will also conduct detailed research. They will scan media for financial statements and announcements, anything that will confirm wealth and whether there is someone who will pay a ransom. Therefore, it makes sense to limit your personal exposure on public media as much as you can.

Stage 3

At this stage the potential target list has been whittled down further and there are few people on it. The kidnappers will now conduct more detailed risk analysis of the remaining potential targets.

They will continue with surveillance and try to determine who will be the easiest to kidnap; who will offer the most reward for the least risk. In most cases this will be the person who is the least security aware, who has the most reliable routines, and potentially who travels to or via locations that could be used for a viable ambush.

Stage 4

The kidnappers have now chosen their final target and they will continue with their planning, able to now focus on the specific details.

They will usually continue with their surveillance which will be more thorough if there are still gaps in their intelligence, but if they already have the information they need they might reign it in somewhat.

They will analyse your movements and the pattern of habits will be re-established. They may take photos or videos of you. They could even practise making the actual kidnapping, albeit in a surreptitious way. Be wary of cars or motorbikes suddenly pulling in front of you, or randomly pulling out suddenly in front of you from a parked position, side street or driveway; or the young couple with a pram suddenly crossing the road and pausing. It is common in the case of kidnappings or terrorist attacks for the perpetrators to test you to see what your reactions and tactics are in certain situations.

They will select from your routine the one time and place for the ambush that has the highest chance of success. For example it could be as you leave your home in the morning, or as you arrive at a particular intersection, or as you stop to wait for the barrier in your gym car park to open.

The kidnappers will find your weak spot and hit you there. We can say for certain that if you are the final target they will choose a location where they are one hundred percent sure you will be, and at a time they know for sure you will be there.

Surveillance

In the previous chapter you learned about the four stages of the kidnap selection process. Hopefully it should have raised many questions because whilst I outlined the process I did not include commentary on how they will conduct surveillance against you, how you can detect it, and what you can do if you suspect you are under surveillance.

Let us start with what information the kidnappers will be gathering with you under surveillance. They will require all information regarding your home and place of work. Can they park up directly outside your house, is it on the street or in its own compound; is it gated? Similarly with your office: are there security guards, is there a professional CCTV system, is it a multi-tenanted building, do you park in the same place every day; do you have an allocated and signposted parking spot?

They will look at the terrain that your home and office is in, and any other place they know you go. Is your home in a rural area and your office in an urban one? Are there places that they can park up or hang around without being noticed? For example if the initial route from the home to the office is primarily a narrow country lane then perhaps they will have to have a man in a field in camouflage rather than a car parked in a narrow urban busy lane that will be noticeable.

As well as places from where they can surveil you, they will also be looking at places for the actual kidnap; the place for the effective ambush. This could be at the end of your driveway whilst you are waiting to turn into traffic on the road; waiting in the road after you come home for your gates to open, or after the sharp bend in the narrow road that you always slow down for.

They will also be looking for their escape routes. It may be that one of the choke points where they can get you is whilst you are parking your car at work, but if people will see the kidnap then the kidnappers are unlikely to get far if it is the middle of rush hour and the office is in the city centre.

The vehicle you drive will be taken into consideration. Do you drive a little electric car, a powerful saloon, or a large SUV? This is especially so if they are thinking of a vehicular ambush as they will need blocking vehicles superior to yours. Also, if you have a 4x4 and they intend to ambush you on a country lane surrounded by fields perhaps you will be able to escape off-road, which they will have to cater for. Perhaps if you cycle to work on certain days then that will provide them with an easier option. Maybe you take public transport and they will have to grab you off the street, or if you use a particular taxi firm maybe they can impersonate a driver.

Again, they will have in-depth knowledge of all the routes they know you use to your primary and secondary locations. Are there one way streets, traffic lights, blind curves or narrow roads? Is there street CCTV? In London there are CCTV cameras with automatic number plate recognition software so that Transport for London can automatically levy their Congestion Charge for driving into certain areas. There is currently a consultation as to whether to allow the Police access to footage from these cameras to aid crime detection. Such things will be in the forefront of the professional kidnappers mind and will help formulate the plan.

The biggest threat against you is your routine; it is the most important information about you that the kidnappers need to know. Case studies of successful kidnaps are testament to this. The kidnappers' analysis of your everyday behaviour will help them decide whether you are a hard or soft target. Obviously, the more predictable you are the easier it is for them.

It should go without saying that your situational awareness is also very important to the kidnappers. If you follow the advice in the *Security in the Street* and *Security in the Vehicle* sections then anyone watching you will hopefully see that you implement security tactics in your day to day life and are therefore a harder target. The kidnappers will have to work harder if you are alert, conscientious and careful.

The places you go or frequent will give the kidnappers a lot of information. Do not think that surveillance is limited to people hiding in fields or cars, or waiting at bus stops. Surveillance could follow you into places you frequent to try and find out more about your routines or how secure the places you go are, and whether anything in that area could be to the kidnapper's advantage.

A kidnapper could follow you into your hairdresser or barber shop, have a haircut whilst you are there and eavesdrop on your conversation, or perhaps befriend the hairdresser. They could be sitting in a restaurant that they know from your routine you go to every Sunday at 2pm. They could be having coffee in the Starbucks around the time they know you get there every Tuesday at 11am. They will dress accordingly. They will fit in. And if they do not, then you would have noticed them and hopefully your suspicions would be raised so that next time you see them you will start to notice a pattern yourself.

Types of Surveillance

Before we move on to discuss how to detect if you are under surveillance let us briefly look at the actual methods of surveillance that exist.

Essentially, there are five classifications: Fixed, Moving, Technical, Combination and Progressive.

Fixed surveillance is where the kidnappers locate themselves in a static location, either renting an apartment or office with an accommodating view, or perhaps parked in a car, or maybe even a street vendor's cart. Ideally the position will afford them views of your entrances and exits. It should go without saying that the kidnappers will want to blend in and not attract attention to themselves.

Moving surveillance is when the kidnappers are following you because you are travelling between locations. This could be by foot or in a vehicle, or both. It is impossible for one person to monitor you for extended periods of time because he will get noticed eventually (unless you are in Condition White!). This means that the team will have to consist of several people.

Understand that the harder the target you are, whether through awareness or unpredictability, or hopefully both, that it will take even more resources to surveil you.

Having a large team makes it easier to follow someone but it also creates complications. They need to communicate with each other so look out for radio usage and earpieces, or people talking on their phone, or eye contact or hand signals between apparently non-associated people. To follow someone professionally takes a lot of training and is not easy to do.

A foot surveillance team will need a minimum of three people to cover you professionally and that also depends on the environment and how hard it is to maintain concealment. Vehicle surveillance is generally much harder to achieve, especially against a "surveillance aware" target, and several vehicles would be needed to remain undetected.

Technical surveillance is when electronic devices are used either to conduct surveillance or assist with it. This could be in the form of battery operated GPS locators secreted under the body of a car, or mini wireless cameras installed in trees, on lampposts, hidden in trash bags (the list is endless) to view the home or office, or even bugging equipment to listen in to conversations that might help provide information about your schedule.

Combination surveillance is generally what you will be up against in most circumstances. It is just a combination of Fixed, Moving and Technical. This usually provides the best results because it allows the kidnapper to change his own "routine" in collecting information. You thought someone was following you on foot the last two days but you haven't seen him for a while because the kidnappers decided to follow you by motorbike or car. Or your house is now under electronic observation, allowing the kidnappers to withdraw surveillance from your immediate locale, reducing their exposure, and they can pick you up at a random intersection and be harder to detect.

Progressive surveillance is the hardest to detect but also the hardest to employ. It is generally only used against a very aware target but it is very demanding on the kidnappers' resources.

It starts off with the kidnapper following you from your home to a particular point along your journey (they may not know where you are going at this stage), at which time they cease the surveillance in case you spot them. The next day they will commence the surveillance from the cease point of the day before and only follow you until a certain point whereby they cut off again and resume another day.

If you are varying your routine, using different vehicles, leaving at different times and taking different routes then this means surveillance will be hugely time consuming for the kidnappers. They may not have the time or the resources for such an activity, and if they are using this method it is because they have flagged you as a hard target so

126

hopefully they will give up and find someone easier!

Surveillance is very expensive and it is very time consuming. The harder the target you are the less likely you are to be kidnapped because the kidnappers most likely will not have sufficient resources to keep you under surveillance.

Detecting Surveillance

We have now looked at the information the kidnappers will want to know and a little bit about the means they can employ to acquire it. This will help you to detect any surveillance against you.

The majority of kidnappings (and assassinations) in the past have taken place within a radius of approximately 500 metres from the victims primary locations and they are usually vehicle based. Primary locations are usually your home and your place of work; the two main fixed locations in your day-to-day schedule.

Be intimately familiar with the immediate areas around your primary locations. Spot anything that looks out of place. Kidnappers will try to blend in to the surrounding anonymity but that is not necessarily so easy. The more familiar you are with your area the easier it will be to spot vehicles or people that potentially do not belong.

To put the above into perspective, imagine you are approaching your house and your neighbour's car that is always parked in a particular spot is suddenly parked elsewhere; you would notice it. If you park in an underground car park at your home or work and one day there is a van or small truck parked where nobody normally parks, you will notice it. If you drive out of your office car park and see a random guy leaning up against a wall where nobody usually stands, you should notice it.

When looking at people in the street or places you go with some regularity, look at the faces of the people around you to see if you recognise them. A person following you will want to change their appearance to avoid being seen. They could put a hat on, take their coat off, or wear sunglasses; they could be carrying a shopping bag that they then dispose of. What they generally do not change is shoes and watches or jewellery which is something you can try and take particular notice of.

Whilst people on foot can change their appearance quite dramatically and easily, the same cannot be said for vehicles. It is true that nowadays many vehicles look similar especially in the dark, but during the daytime it is hard to change the profile of a vehicle, or its colour.

Pay particular attention to rental vehicles. Although renting cars will leave a trace for police to eventually follow it provides the kidnappers with potentially numerous different cars. Renting cars means that they can swap cars frequently enough so that you are less likely to notice any car in particular. If you do notice a car they may have changed it within a few hours or a couple of days making it harder for you to determine whether you are under surveillance. Always make a note of your suspicions (the same car may be back a few days later) and obviously if you see a series of rental cars then that should be cause for concern. Pay attention to vehicles with foreign plates as well, and also to signs of communications such as extra or temporary antennas stuck on the outside.

When walking in the street, you can vary your pace. You can increase speed to see if anyone tries to keep up or you can slow down to see if someone maintains their distance. However you should always try to do this in a calm manner, and not be erratic in your method. You have to act a little, and pretend you are slowing down to look in shops, or to read something on your phone (but not if you think you are about to be the subject of a mugging).

Stopping to look in shop windows is a good opportunity to take stock of a situation. You can possibly use the reflection in the window to see who is approaching, but it also gives you the opportunity to look around you and actually "see" what is there rather than trying to do that whilst walking in the opposite direction.

Try to see who is walking on the other side of the street; people conducting surveillance against you will do their upmost to be discreet and not be seen by you at all. They will also want to avoid eye contact as much as possible because when direct eye contact is made you are more likely to remember that face.

Suddenly patting your packets and pretending you have forgotten something is a good way to have an excuse to turn around and head back in the direction you just came from. You now have the perfect way to scan the faces of the people coming towards you. A professional tail will just continue straight past you but untrained people might react in a way that will raise suspicions: they could duck into a doorway, suddenly turn and face a shop, turn and follow you directly, or signal or glance to another member of their team to take over.

If you are in a shopping mall or transportation system where there are escalators, you can walk up part of the way and then just stop, turn and face the direction you have just come from and observe the people behind you. It gives you a good amount of time to casually scan faces and see if you recognise anyone. Even if you do not recognise anyone, and you are being followed, the surveillance team will see that you are practising some counter surveillance.

You can go into a store and browse items whilst observing who comes in after you. Entering venues is a big decision for any surveillance people as it could expose them quite easily to you. However, waiting around outside could have its limitations as there might not be anywhere to casually wait around and it could unnerve them being so exposed. Before you enter the store try and take a mental picture of places nearby such as cafe's, bus stops and other places someone might wait.

When you leave, pause near the entrance and scan the area to see if there is anything that draws your attention; anything different to how it was before you went in. If you think someone actually followed you into the store, now would be a good time to decide to go back in to "make that purchase" that you were deliberating over, and as you walk back in you can see if anyone was following you out. It is more likely that someone followed you into the store if it was a large place with multiple exits.

You could intentionally walk into a small coffee shop and see if anyone enters with you and suddenly realises they are exposed. You could enter the same shop and take a table by the window. You could walk past said coffee shop a few metres, turn around, scan the area, then go into the coffee shop and sit by the window and see if you can identify anyone that you recognise or anyone reacting to the situation you have created. Will the person following you come in and sit down, or will they find an observation post nearby, or will you see someone communicating either in person or by phone or radio from your vantage point?

Similarly, when you go to eat in a restaurant you should choose a seat that affords you a good view of who enters the establishment. A lot of people seem to do this, whether under threat of kidnap or not, just because they like to see what is going on around them and so that they have more time to react. Some people are just naturally uncomfortable sitting in a venue with their back to the door; they feel exposed.

I will add to the above, because there are other scenarios that you should take into consideration. Firstly, check if there are other entrances and exits. This goes for the kitchen as well. People tend to forget that pretty much all restaurants have a rear entrance. So, when you choose your seat, try and commandeer one that gives you a view of as much of the restaurant as possible, encompassing the kitchen entrance to the restaurant as well as the front door.

If this restaurant is part of your routine then understand that perhaps this week your kidnappers are already inside having their meal, just to observe, for thoroughness, so if you are sitting facing the door, make sure you have had a quick scan of other patrons already seated.

You are less likely to be kidnapped from a public place. However, if you have a habit of always going to that restaurant on a Thursday night, and you have a habit of going to the restroom before you leave, and the restroom happens to be out of sight, at the rear, adjacent to the unsecured rear exit, then understand that you are in a compromised location. So, be intimately familiar with the places you frequent, and be aware of the people around you.

We are not covering terrorism in this book but using the restaurant scenario, know your exits and possibly consider trying to find your ultimate seat that provides you with a good view of the comings and goings through the main entrance and the kitchen but also giving you quick access to an exit in case of a terrorist attack.

If you do enter a coffee shop or restaurant, consider paying at time of ordering, so that you can get up and leave quickly. This can catch out someone conducting surveillance and you may see signs that they try to pay quickly as they will now be in a hurry to leave.

When taking public transport such as buses and trains, you can use a similar tactic to determine if you are being followed. You can get on the bus or train, and just before it pulls away or the doors close, you can alight again and see who gets off. You can then wait for the next one and see if they follow.

You might be reading this and starting to think that perhaps these "counter surveillance" tactics that will help you determine if you are under surveillance could actually expose you to more imminent danger. For example, if you do get on a bus and then jump off, catching the surveillance person unawares and causing him to expose himself, you do not know how he will react if you are suddenly both standing in an empty street or on an empty platform.

So try to make sure that any action you take will be subtle. You got off the bus because you patted your pocket, couldn't find your phone, panicked and jumped off to retrace your steps. Or you have realised that you got on the wrong bus or train and you need to be going the other way. Act it out and try not to be acting like a spy that is actively avoiding known pursuers.

There are certain people in this world that use these measures with frequency. Not necessarily to determine if someone is following them, but just to make it harder in case someone is following them. This is really "anti-surveillance": just being a hard target. This is fairly easy to do because you just act in a random way, making sporadic changes to direction, transportation and supposed destination.

Counter surveillance, which is what we are discussing in this chapter, is much harder. So if for any reason you do feel that you are under some surveillance, you should always report it to the local authorities. If, for various reasons that is not an option, or they do not have the resources to assist you, you can always use colleagues or friends to assist you in determining if you are being followed.

You still use the tactics already discussed, but instead of you paying attention to the area and people potentially following you, you have others to do that for you. You can set up what is referred to as a Surveillance Detection Route. This will involve planning a walking route through a certain area and at key locations you have your friend(s) observing to see who, if anyone, is following you.

You can choose a small area involving, for example, a 20 minute walk that passes by two or three locations such as coffee shops, bus stops, any place someone can unobtrusively wait. Obviously, if you are using a different lookout at each position then it will be harder to determine if the same person or people are following you unless your lookouts are videoing the people as they walk by after you. You will have to sit with them afterwards and see what notes they made and review the footage.

If you only have one person to assist you then plan a route that enables your lookout to leave the first position and get to the second before you. It helps if you begin in a high-density area and then walk to an area that is far less populated. Take an indirect route so that you can, to the best of your ability,

134

rule out picking up someone that just happens to be taking the same route as you from A to B. In theory, if you have three choke points of your own and you have chosen them so that they are not just in a straight line, then anyone near you at all three locations should be treated as suspicious.

A surveillance detection route can be vehicle-based too. This is easier to achieve because your friends can just be sitting in a car at a particular point observing, and it is easier to drive to the second and third choke points. You can also conduct your own surveillance detection route: just by driving a pre-planned route and seeing if there are any vehicles behind you at all. Again, driving from a populated area to one of little activity is the best way to achieve this.

To aid the above you can consider perhaps making a turn without signalling, or signalling late to see if someone starts to signal after, or who also turns without signalling. You can go through a traffic light just before it changes to see if anyone else follows. You can pull over somewhere to see if a car pulls in further behind. If you know areas where there are street cameras then this would be a good place to try this so that if you are reporting these activities to the authorities then they will have video footage. You can also drive into a petrol forecourt, potentially to buy petrol, food from the store, or just to pull over for a few minutes whilst you make a call. I use the example of a petrol station because although they are quite anonymous, they are usually very busy and often have comprehensive surveillance-camera coverage.

If you do find yourself under surveillance you must change your routines.

Surprise, Surprise, Surprise

We have now discussed various methods you can employ, either on your own or with friends or colleagues, to detect if you are under surveillance. However there are some points that we have touched on that need to be reinforced and elaborated on.

For a kidnapper to successfully kidnap you he will require surprise. For him to have the element of surprise he will have had to conduct detailed surveillance on you. Ergo, if you have detected the surveillance you will be aware and you will be unsurprisable. This should mean that the kidnappers will move on to a different target.

Remember how much emphasis I put on "awareness" in the early chapters of the book. Regardless of the type of attack, an attacker requires surprise in order to make an effective attack against you. Kidnapping is no different. If you are someone who could be under threat then it goes without saying that you should be in Condition Yellow at all times.

I mentioned that most kidnappings happen within 500 metres of your home or office. Of those two locations, the home is the higher risk. This is because most people leave their home at specific times. They obviously also may arrive at work at specific times but there could be meetings out of the office, and many other reasons that make this location not the first choice for the attempt.

Generally, most people are at their most relaxed when in these areas — they are familiar with them and feel "at home". It goes without saying therefore, that you need to ramp up your levels of awareness when arriving and departing these locations.

When you leave your home or office the options open to you are usually fairly limited to a left or right turn, and usually you take the same route every day. As you get further away from these locations the route options expand and so the likelihood of being attacked at that stage is significantly reduced.

Out of all the factors that kidnappers take into consideration when planning a kidnap, such as location, transportation and weapons, the most important is time; the time when they know for sure where you will be. We have said that it is important to change routines, including changing driving routes, but this is not always easy to achieve. Being on time for work is a hard habit to break which in essence means that we may be making it easier for the kidnappers to plan.

However, if it is hard for you to be unpredictable then it will be hard for the kidnappers to be inconspicuous during the surveillance. So you need to develop an early warning system and monitor "abnormal" activity near your home and office. This is not very hard and doesn't take much effort; you probably already do it subconsciously.

Without realising it you most likely know what cars belong in your immediate neighbourhood, what times kids are taken to school, what time the

UPS man delivers; the general patterns of the area. This is a natural phenomenon — you have a mental image of what you see, which helps you to understand when something is out of place or unusual.

If someone or something is seen in your area that is not usually there, then you will notice it — especially if you are in Condition Yellow. Always question, always doubt. Why is that utility truck there? Are those the normal gardeners working across the street? Why are two people sitting in that car down the road?

Everyone at some time or another has left home and seen something that does not belong. Your awareness level must be raised to a point where:

Strange vehicles parked in the vicinity are noticed and reported to the authorities or your security department. It may be the first time you have seen the vehicle but it may not be the first time it was there. You do not know what stage of planning the kidnappers are up to – it could be Stage 2 surveillance or it could be that they are in the final stages;

You have noticed strange people hanging around, sitting, walking, or perhaps partaking in an unusual activity or no activity at all;

You have noticed that you are being followed. Keep a note of any strange sightings. Maybe carry a small recorder, or use your smartphone. Take as much information as you can and include: day, date and time, car make and model, license number, condition of the car, number of occupants and descriptions of the people, if possible. You should make these notes even if you are unsure you are being followed. People have a habit of forgetting things. Keep the recordings or a diary. You might be noticing more suspicious activity than you realise and it will only be by keeping a record that you can quantify and check it.

Remember, a kidnapper requires surprise to kidnap you. Combined with that surprise will be a lot of aggression and possible violence. They will need to shock you into submission. They could come up and politely threaten you to go with them but in all likelihood it will be hard, fast and aggressive. There will be enough of them to control the situation and ensure your complete compliance. They will have chosen the time and the place and have planned it well.

If you can change your routines it will show the kidnappers that you are unpredictable. And it will make it harder for them. Hopefully they will choose an easier target.

I do not know where you are in the world while you are reading this book. Some places have significantly higher rates of kidnappings than others. In some countries kidnapping are so rare they are virtually unheard of; in others it is quite literally a daily occurrence. But wherever you are, understand this: kidnappers are not nice people and they will most likely be brutal. They might hide you in a tiny hole in the floor or ground. They might cut off ears and fingers as proof of their ruthlessness. They send videos of them raping the victim to shock loved ones into paying faster.

In Guatemala, we estimated that 40-50% of kidnap victims were killed by their kidnappers either because the victim, during captivity, found out that they knew the kidnappers, because it had simply become too much trouble, or because they were killed during the kidnap but the body was taken so that the kidnappers could still try and claim the ransom. Try not to get kidnapped!

We have discussed security in various locations, including your home. We haven't discussed the security at your place of employment, which I feel falls slightly outside the scope of this book. The only comment I want to make on it is that assuming your home is secure and you vary your routine, you are making yourself a harder target for kidnapping. But if you have no security in your office and all someone has to do to meet you is call and make an appointment, then this is a security hole that needs to be addressed.

How to Elude Someone Who is Following You

We discussed some options in the *Detecting Surveillance* chapter that will help you detect if you are being followed and tactics that can also be used as "anti-surveillance." For example, taking sporadic random actions that make it difficult for someone to follow you without exposing themselves. The biggest threat to an attacker is the security he cannot see — and maybe you playing the hard target will also make them wonder if anyone is assisting you on the ground with counter surveillance.

But there may come a time when you have detected a pattern of surveillance and for whatever reason you feel that an attack against you is imminent. No one can make this decision for you – it might even just be a gut feeling. If you do have that feeling, the time for subtlety has passed and you must move with a purpose.

We have said before, know the safe havens in your area: police stations, embassies, military installations, government buildings with security; you have to know your area and know where you can go and by what means.

Use high density to your advantage and try and lose them. You can enter and leave crowded buildings using multiple entrances and exits. You must get to a safe place. Try to change the general outline of your appearance after ducking round a corner or going through a throng of people or a doorway. Surveillance people latch on to distinctive parts of you that they can see from a distance so if you were wearing sunglasses and a bright red jacket then take them both off and perhaps put a hat on. You can consider trying to change your height by stooping or hunching your shoulders, or changing your gait or limping.

It may seem obvious but inform your emergency contact or law enforcement of your predicament whilst you are on the move. This is so that they can co-ordinate to pick you up, or at least be aware that you have a situation and are en route to a particular destination. Also they may be able to catch whoever is following you.

If you have the opportunity, get in a taxi and drive straight to a safe haven. In extreme emergencies it might be possible to flag down a passing car although be wary of who is in the car.

If you are driving yourself then understand that you should, if necessary, break any law to get away from the immediate threat and to a safe place. This does not mean running over innocent people but if you have to speed, speed. If you need to jump red lights, do it. If you have to mount the curb or dent a couple of cars, do it. Just try to do it all without panic, and to do it all safely. Try and remain calm and in control.

If you have extricated yourself from the area then do not continue to speed unnecessarily. That said, maintain your awareness until you arrive at your safe haven because if you start to relax after an intense adrenalin-fuelled action, your body will have come down from its high and if you are suddenly attacked you will struggle to positively react and you are more likely to crumble.

If driving, try to stay on wide, major roads. If you can take a road with less traffic and fewer traffic lights then even better. Keep checking your mirrors to see if the suspicious vehicle is still with you. You can potentially conduct a quick surveillance detection route but at this stage it is not recommended and you are far better to focus on getting to your safe haven as quickly as possible.

Understand that if there is a car following you, it might not be anything sinister at all – it might just be a coincidence. That said, it could be the final stage of the kidnappers plan, or it could be an over exuberant surveillance person who has forgotten that he was supposed to remain covert. You will not know. Get to the safe haven.

Remember though, for the most part, kidnappers do not want to get caught and they do not want to try and grab a hard target, least of all one that has identified he is under surveillance and taking decisive action to escape. However, there are always exceptions to that rule. There are some people in the world that are missing the "fear of consequence" gene, and they will do things that defy all logic.

Look at the Somali pirates. They know there are international military task forces trying to stop them. They know that many ships have armed guards and quite serious counter measures, yet they still persist. So my point is that although I have repeatedly said that attackers in general, and especially kidnappers, need surprise, that with the element of surprise lost they may still try and regain control of the situation. So be wary.

It is possible that some very intelligent people orchestrated the kidnapping, but the foot soldiers doing the collection are not too smart. You resist, they forget that there has been months of planning, and they kill you "by mistake" whilst you are trying to escape.

If you are relaying information by phone whilst driving try to use a hands-free device or the built-in speaker on the phone. You want both hands on the steering wheel. Focus on the driving and not on the talking, but keep the line open if you can for updates.

143

Again, know where you are going and do not take sudden random side streets that may result in you trapping yourself in a dead end or narrow street with a truck coming the opposite way. You will end up ambushing yourself.

If you know for sure that someone is following you then again, head directly to a safe haven. Taking a step back, if you now feel that it is not a pending attack then you can continue with some surveillance detection. Vary your speed to see if the vehicle maintains the same distance between you. Change lanes and see his reaction. Circle a roundabout a few times and see if the car is still there. Take a late exit from a highway and see if the car follows. If it was surveillance it is unlikely to still be following you – they would have pulled off to resume another time. If the car is still there you should clearly be concerned.

If you are on a highway then consider driving on the inside lane, at a moderate speed, and see who drives past. If you are on a highway or motorway and drive just below the speed limit it is very unlikely that someone will stay behind you.

If someone else is driving, the endangered person could always lie down in the car after going around a bend or when out of sight from the tailing car, to give the impression that he managed to get out, to confuse the people following.

The Ambush

We have covered a lot of information in this kidnap section but we have not yet discussed real life incidents. Whenever there is an attack, it is good to find out as much about it as possible and write a case study that you can pick apart with friends or colleagues. Studying real attacks or kidnappings opens your mind to the types of ambushes you might be faced with, and you can work out counter measures for dealing with it. I am not going to cite specific case studies here but I will give some examples of how some ambushes have and could be made.

Be aware at pedestrian crossings, or any road location, where there is a woman with a pram crossing the road. There may not necessarily be a baby in the pram. If you slow down and stop to let them cross the woman could block your path with the pram, and the attackers could come from the side when you are unaware, point weapons at you and kidnap you. Or without hot weapons (i.e. firearms) they could smash through your side windows with a hammer to the same result. If you are untrained you will panic. You might not want to go forwards because in your subconscious you will not want to kill the baby. You cannot reverse because traffic is stacked up already. In that situation, understand that it is very unlikely that there is a baby in the pram, and you can always nudge it out the way before accelerating away. But yes, the attackers will still be trying to get in. Hands will be on you. If they have hot weapons then you need to move as fast as you can.

There was a real incident whereby a wealthy businessman was ambushed in his car. His driver slowed down and stopped for a vehicle that was blocking their path. Another car came from behind and blocked them in. Gunmen appeared, carrying a heavy hammer. The car was armoured but the armoured glass was not embedded enough into the upper part of the sill. They used the hammer to crack the armour and peel it away. They put a gun through the window and shot the driver and then kidnapped the businessman.

Could this have been avoided? Unfortunately, yes. The driver was not trained in security driving. He stalled the car after he stopped and did not know what to do. He could have driven around the ambush or even rammed it out of the way. Unfortunately he did not do anything and paid the ultimate price. If you do have the luxury of an armoured car, use it to your advantage and know that you have time to escape before the armour is breached. Do not just sit there – no armour is impenetrable and it is not designed to withstand repeat attacks to the same area.

Be aware of motorcycles with pillion passengers riding offset to your vehicle. This is a very popular means of ambush and assassination. Motorcycles are powerful and highly mobile, and someone on the back is free to shoot or place an explosive device on the car. Motorcycles however are very vulnerable especially when moving; if you enrol on an anti-ambush driving course perhaps it is something you can discuss with your instructor.

In some countries you get people selling flowers or cleaning windscreens at traffic lights. Be extremely wary of any such person, especially if they approach your vehicle. Always hang back away from them even if it means leaving 10 metres of road between you and the car in front. As said in the *Security in the Street* section, do not enter their predetermined "kill zone". Stay away, give yourself distance and time to react.

As with the above situation at traffic lights and junctions, kidnappers could utilise children as a distraction. Likewise, there could be a staged accident. You may think that this sounds like something from the movies but it is a distinct possibility, as are fake road-works and diversions. Always slow down, evaluate, and give yourself time to turn around and take a different route.

Do not forget, even if you are unarmed you still have a weapon: your vehicle. It is fast, powerful and heavy. It can be used against people and to shunt vehicles out of the way (if used correctly).

Remember, an ambush is unlikely to be conducted by one person acting alone. There are likely to be several members of the team, some for distraction, some for the attack and some for the extraction. They will have planned to shock you in to submission at a time and place of their choosing. We now know the likely places for these types of attacks so it is up to you to be aware when near them.

After concluding this type of course in countries where kidnapping was a daily occurrence, people would ask "When I leave here now, if I see a car that seems to be following me, how will I know if they are conducting surveillance or if the kidnapping is imminent?". Unfortunately, there is no way to know. It is a scary world sometimes.

Security in Transit

I would like to spend a bit of time going through some tactics for when you are travelling on public transport or by taxi. We have already covered a lot of tactics in the *Street* and *Vehicle* sections but now that we have finished the *Kidnap Prevention* element and you are probably looking for surveillance everywhere, I think this is a good time to take a step away from that and discuss something a bit less daunting.

Trains

Trains are a popular means of transport, either for work or travel. In some cities trains run all night and if they do not, they certainly run from very early in the morning to very late at night. Whether you take an underground or overground train the principles and threats are generally the same.

Statistically, compared with the amount of commuters, it is unlikely that you will experience a violent crime on a train however in today's day and age with every type of person from every type of place mixing in one city, anything can happen.

Exactly the same types of crimes can happen to you on a train as in the *Street*. When you are on the platform, be aware of who is around you. If you see someone that looks problematic then reposition yourself further away. Also, as a general rule, get into the habit of not standing near the platform edge, just in case there is some kind of commotion when the train is arriving and you get pushed on to the tracks.

149

Do not get into the same carriage with someone who seems to be drunk or suspicious. When you get on the train, don't take the first seat you see but scan the area. If there are a loud bunch of drunks or aggressive looking people then clearly that is not where you want to sit. I fully realise that on a busy commute you will just want to sit anywhere but bear in mind that generally no one will help you if a problem develops, so it is always better to distance yourself from a potential threat.

Trains have different designs but generally are split into carriages. Carriages often have a mix of single and double exit doors. Try and sit near one of the exit doors in case you need to get up and get out quickly. Sitting near the double doors might afford you a better escape route as the corridor area is usually wider so there is more room to manoeuvre if the area is congested.

Know where the emergency lever is to alert the driver if you are in trouble. Always use it as soon as you can. This could help in the same way as the woman pressing her panic button in her home when she was about to be raped as mentioned in the *Security in the Home* section.

Some seats on trains have partitions next to them separating the standing area. If you have travelled on the London Underground you will know what I am referring to. Sitting in one of these seats gives you partial protection from an assailant as they will only be able to attack you from the front and one of the sides as you will have the partition on the other. These seats also happen to be near the doors, so if you were attacked or had a situation develop, you could consider launching yourself off your seat and out the door quite quickly if you were at a platform. The emergency levers are also usually by the doors so if the doors weren't open you could use the lever to alert the driver.

Many trains have interconnecting doors which can be used whilst the train is in motion, albeit with care. So if you see a situation developing, not necessarily against you, you can leave the carriage.

When travelling at night, or if your journey takes you through dangerous areas, or at times when there are not a lot of passengers around, sit in the carriage near the driver, or near the guard or conductor if there is one.

Sexual assault on trains can be an issue. There are lots of predators in the world, and also opportunists. When standing in cramped conditions on a busy train someone may take advantage. Obviously this mostly applies to women but can also apply to men (and of course to children as well). If someone is touching you then you must move away. Do not be shy about it. Do not be intimidated. In most cases it would be better to vocalise what is happening and shout something to attract attention such as "Keep away from me". "Stop touching me". "Help, he is assaulting me". If you have the training and temerity to do it, turn around and see who the predator is. Knee him in the groin. Head-butt him. Poke your fingers into his windpipe at the base of the neck. Be morally indignant. No one has a right to touch you. Try not to let fear take over; do not just stand there and let it happen.

I was at a seminar recently where an instructor discussed how women perceive things differently to men, and how women are more uncomfortable when in close proximity to an unknown man compared to how a man feels in close proximity to an unknown woman. A simple test was done with men standing near women, moving closer and closer towards the women to see how close they got before the women were in so much discomfort that they had to shout "stop". They then reversed the test to see how close the men would let the women approach before they felt uncomfortable. In most cases the women felt far more uncomfortable much earlier than the men.

This test went some way to show that on a busy train, a man would be happier to stand close to a woman and not be perturbed by it, whilst the woman could be feeling intensely uncomfortable. If the man then tried to engage the woman in conversation, or came unacceptably close, the women said that they would relocate themselves to a different part of the train, especially if it was less populated, which should be a clear message to the man that he should keep away. The instructor gave the man's view, albeit it would have to be a slightly deranged man in my opinion. The man sees the woman go to a quiet area of the train and thinks "Oh cool, she has gone somewhere quiet for me to go and be alone with her". So now the woman is perhaps in a more vulnerable position than she was initially.

The point of this is to say that if you are feeling intimidated in that kind of situation, unless you can move to a confirmed safer area then a better approach would be to politely say to the man "Excuse me, but I feel uncomfortable when people are standing so close to me". Communicate politely but be clear. Don't forget "the fence" tactics that we learned about in the *Dialogue and Distance* of the *Street* section; use your arms and hands (and even luggage or large bag if you have one with you) to create some distance between you.

When on intercity trains with toilets and other possibly secluded areas, be aware of people hanging around them when you pass by or go to use the facilities. If in doubt, get a guard to wait, or come back later on, or find another toilet.

It should go without saying that when you reach your destination that you should take basic steps to ensure that no one followed you off the train. Such a person could walk ahead and leave the station before you so that you feel that there is no danger to be concerned about, so be aware also when leaving the station. Pay attention to the people around you.

Buses

Much of what has been written in the train section will apply to buses but there are some differences and additions. Try to sit on the lower deck of a bus, near to one of the exits. Buses stop a lot more frequently and are usually slow moving due to traffic. If there is an incident on the bus, know where the door override controls are so that you can evacuate yourself if need be. Try to take a seat that affords you a good view of people getting on or at least in a place where if possible your back is not exposed to too many people.

Unlike trains that stop in stations that are usually very well illuminated and also covered by extensive camera surveillance systems, buses tend to stop in the street which automatically puts you in a more vulnerable position. Always take a moment to scan the area when you get off and make sure you are not walking into a hostile situation.

If you get off the bus and you think someone followed you off, wait at the bus stop until that person has moved out of sight. Call for a cab or someone to pick you up if you are concerned, or even make that pretend call saying, "Hi, yep, I'm at the bus stop, see you in 2 minutes".

Never walk off in a panic with someone following you. You will become more scared and eventually crumble if they attack or force you to go somewhere with them.

Taxis

In most countries taxis are licensed. But of course there are always unlicensed taxis looking to offer cheaper fares. Avoid them. If you are ordering a taxi by phone or by App, make sure it is from a reputable and reliable firm and check that you are getting into the correct vehicle when it arrives. Taxi rapes are very common all over world.

Try to have some understanding and awareness of your route in case the driver is diverting to another location. Always let someone know you are taking a taxi and from where to where and with which firm, just in case.

Be aware of taxi muggings, especially from airports. In some countries it is common for a traveller to jump into a taxi at an airport, and a few hundred metres into the journey the driver pulls over and an accomplice jumps in and steals the traveller's belongings at gunpoint. In many cases, there is significant violence shown towards the traveller. Understand that this ploy can also work for abductions and kidnappings, which you can understand from reading the previous *Kidnap Prevention* section.

Express Kidnappings

In some countries, especially those with many illegal or unlicensed taxis, poor law enforcement and corrupt officials, you need to aware of "express kidnappings." This is when you are picked up in a taxi, and similarly to the situation mentioned above, an accomplice (or several) joins you in the cab and you are taken on a tour of ATM machines to withdraw as much money as possible. This could also develop into the assailants taking you to your home to rob it (unless you are a tourist). Understand that this type of crime as previously said can also lead to sexual assault. Try to always use reputable firms.

When travelling overseas, before you leave always take a look at the US or UK Foreign Office travel advisory websites. The information they provide is usually very accurate and current and will help you to understand the potential dangers of the country or city you are travelling to, which in turn will help you keep safe.

Mental Blueprints

As you go about your daily life, you should occasionally think through attack situations; anticipate how an attack might unfold and how you can avoid it, or what reactions you can make if you are unable to avoid it. The more you think about different dangerous scenarios and encounters, and think through the options available to you, the more likely you are to make a positive reaction when attacked.

To use a simple but realistic example, if you think that you could be attacked when leaving for work in the morning, when you are super sleepy and unaware, think through the scenario that you have unlocked and opened your front door, and as you step outside your attacker steps into your line of sight. Let us say for arguments sake that you know for sure he is there to attack you, so you very quickly retreat back inside, close the door, lock all the locks, and call the Police.

You can build things in to that scenario; the attacker was too close for you to get inside without him grabbing you, so you pushed him backwards, or picked up the plant pot you have on your porch and smashed it over his head.

Pulling up at traffic lights you notice someone walking along the pavement that looks suspicious. You know your doors are locked and your windows are up so you are not unduly concerned. But you are thinking about what if he pulls out a hammer to shatter your side window to open your door to jump in. As a habit you now leave manoeuvrable space in front but there is a car blocking you to the side and you cannot pull out, so you can think to drive forward into your manoeuvrable space. If the attacker follows you, and if the car behind has not driven forwards with you, you can reverse back again. Your hand is on the horn attracting attention whilst you are driving back and forth. The lights change and you drive away, or perhaps the threat was so severe that you mount the curb and drive around the lights.

There is a man walking towards you. You think to yourself what you would do if he tries to grab your bag and run. It is difficult because it is strapped to you. But the man might punch you, so you've decided that you will grab him by the head with both hands and launch forward with maximum aggression and drive his head into the glass store front next to you. You will then jump into the taxi that you have seen coming down the road, knowing there is no traffic and you will have a potentially seamless escape.

The more you think the more likely you are to make a reaction. By thinking through all these "what ifs" you will create plans, or mental blueprints that will help you to react much faster. Even something simple: you are sitting in your car waiting for a friend. You see a man walking over to your car with a look of intent. Because you are trained you have the engine running, the doors locked, space to drive off, and so you do just that. No effort, no drama, and you are out of the danger area.

Remember, any reaction is usually better than no reaction at all, so even if your initial response was not effective, because you did actually react you will now have the impetus to continue and adapt, making decisions that are more appropriate to the situation you are in.

With your situational Condition Yellow awareness, try to pay attention to items that you see in the street or around you at any location that could be used to your benefit as an improvised weapon. It could be a brick by a wall that you can throw at an attacker or club round the head with; it could be a metal bar or chair leg lying in a skip that you can use to defend yourself against a knife-wielding attacker; it could be a chair in a restaurant for a similar purpose. The list is endless.

In most cases, after being attacked you will want to report it to the authorities, especially if you had to flee the scene of the attack before the police arrive. You should do this as soon as you possibly can so that hopefully the perpetrator(s) can be arrested, and also so that you can give your side of the story first. There are some situations or countries in which you will not want to report the crime but this is a decision only you can make for yourself after carefully considering the risk.

Combat

Unarmed

If you are concerned for your safety I strongly recommend enrolling in a good unarmed combat course, or classes. My personal view is that on-going classes do not suit most people's lifestyles, at least not beyond the short term, so if you can participate in a short course with predefined goals, then do that. It is a lot easier to fit in to your life than trying to give up a couple of evenings a week "forever". You can always do more courses or refresher classes.

Initially you only need to learn some basic techniques such as straight punches, hooks, elbow strikes, hammer strikes, knee strikes, blocks and possibly groin kicks. Other types of kicks are generally redundant in street attacks and although it is always good to learn them, not at the expense of the tools you are more likely to need.

Learning these "basics" will enhance your awareness and give you confidence. Once you have those skills, depending on your perceived needs then you should learn some effective defences against knife attacks. If you are in a country or area that has a lot of gun crime then you should implement weapon disarms in to your training as well.

It is imperative to develop your physical aggression and mental determination and you need to be in classes that pressure test those techniques in simulated real life situations. Understand that some fights will develop from an argument where there was no pre-fight fear or concern and it just escalates gradually. Other attacks could be fearsome – someone might threaten you from across the street and run over to attack you. During that time you will have an adrenal dump, your heart will be thumping and you might feel yourself getting terrified. There is nothing wrong with fear; everyone will be scared in that situation. But you need to try and channel it into cold aggression. Training will help you achieve that.

When researching a place to train, or an instructor to teach you, do not confuse Martial Arts with self defence, combatives or reality-based fighting. Martial Arts are great if you have years to invest in training, but even then, they do not really address street defence and the types of attacks you may face day to day. You can usually learn more about how to defend yourself in 6 hours of Krav Maga or another reality-based combative system than you will in 6 months or even years in a traditional Martial Art.

Armed

If you live in a country where it is legal to carry a pistol, or you can have one at home for self defence, or if you have a shotgun, you should know how to use it. Knowing how to use it is not the same as going to the range once a year, calmly loading the magazine and shooting at a target in your own relaxed time. You should do a shooting course that teaches you how to shoot under pressure, how to vary rates of fire over distance, multiple attackers, changing magazines and so on.

I was a shooting instructor and range master many years ago. Every now and then we did some short courses for civilians. Often people turned up with supreme confidence that they were experts with guns. Generally they could not shoot well at all and after making them run 20 metres and do 20 push ups just to get their hearts pumping, most of them could not hit a man sized target at 7 metres. Some could not even find the target! My point is this: if you carry a gun for your own protection, invest the time to learn how to use it properly, and in pressured scenarios when the adrenalin is flowing.

Online Security

Whilst writing this book one evening I received a random email via a domain I used to have that is now dormant. The email was from an unemployed secretary looking for a job, and included her full name, address and curriculum vitae (resume).

The woman had bought a mailing list which contained an email address that had never actually even existed on my old domain but used the @myemail.co.uk suffix. Because I had a "catchall" account set up the email was sent on to a random Gmail account which flashed up on my Blackberry at 10pm on a Tuesday night.

This kind of thing must happen all the time and will mostly get ignored, blocked or just deleted. But I was curious to find out a little bit more about this secretary so I opened up Facebook and typed in her name. Nothing came up at all. I was going to give up. I wasn't really that interested. But I thought I would try one more thing so I typed in a different spelling of her first name and voila, up came a few matches. On the first page was a picture of one of these women and surprisingly, under the name, an area of London was listed that matched the locale of the woman who sent the email. So I had found her. In less than two minutes. I know her name, her address, what she looks like, and because her Facebook profile was not locked down at all I also understand quite a bit about her character from the posts she has made. Obviously I can also see her friends.

If this woman's email had been inadvertently sent to a sexual deviant, a rapist, a murderer, an extortionist or some other type of sick individual she could potentially be in danger now. Such a person could respond to her email and invite her to a fictitious interview at a random location. Anything could happen to her. I am sitting here wondering whether I should write to her and outline the dangers of being so exposed.

I had never intended to write anything at all about the dangers associated with one's online presence. To be honest, it is not something I particularly want to write about especially because I think the government and other professional bodies are doing quite a good job of raising awareness.

But I had to share that story because there are some people out there who to their detriment, willingly dismiss the risks, or are too naive or too technologically unaware to realise how much of their information is floating around and accessible that could be physically dangerous to them in the wrong hands. I am not talking about cyber crime and ID theft. I am talking real physical trauma.

So, if you have young relatives and they live their lives on social media, make sure they lock things down so that only trusted friends can see their pertinent details. If you have an elderly relative who does not know any better, then it is your job to educate them.

Learning Exercises

When we conduct our Security Awareness & Attack Recognition courses we use some practical and table-top exercises to help the participants understand certain aspects better. If you so wish, together with some family members, friends or colleagues, you can conduct similar exercises to achieve the same goals.

Before conducting any of these exercises, especially the ones taking place in public, always consider the health and safety of all concerned parties, and do not do anything that may be illegal or that will raise unnecessary suspicions.

Exercise 1 - Surveillance on You

I already mentioned that we conduct basic surveillance on some of the participants as they arrive, to show them later on how unaware they are, or at least, how unaware they are of how easy it is for something that might look normal to in fact be not so normal.

This is something you can arrange with relative ease if you are so inclined to do so.

Exercise 2 - Surveillance on You II

On our courses we generally discuss Exercise 1 just before breaking for lunch. It is used to help finish the morning by reinforcing some of the lessons already learned. It is also supposed to cause the participants to elevate their levels of awareness whilst out at lunch.

If we knew where they were dining we would send a couple of people ahead to the restaurant to already be seated. Generally we would send a couple and one single person. We would also send a couple of people to follow the group from our office to the restaurant.

When they came back from lunch we would ask them if they thought they were under surveillance at any time or if they saw anything suspicious. Some people thought they might have been under surveillance because of the nature of the course, but did not see anything; for others it did not occur to them at all.

We would then bring in our helpers and ask the participants if they had ever seen any of them before. They generally hadn't. The helpers then went on to explain where they had been sitting and what they saw, as did the foot followers.

The purpose of the exercise was to demonstrate to them that they really need to be in Condition Yellow and also "see" and not just "look". They should have noticed the people following them even if they did not feel they were suspicious. They should have seen who was sitting adjacent to them at the restaurant – maybe there would have been some awkwardness between the two helpers that the group could have picked up on. The group should have paid attention to the person sitting by himself. Is it unusual for someone to be sitting by themselves – no, but for people under threat they should be looking at every possibility.

You can run similar exercises but it is important that the helpers have clear briefings regarding what to do and how to act.

Exercise 3 – Surveilling Others

After reading this book you should have quite a good understanding about surveillance and if you are a person at risk you may be seeing attackers everywhere (for a week or so!). It is important to put things into perspective. It is not easy to follow someone and it is not easy to find out meaningful information. The person conducting the surveillance, especially if untrained may feel very exposed and extremely nervous.

To help understand this, and in some way for them to understand what they should be looking for themselves when conducting counter-surveillance, we used to take our group out into the street, and in pairs, allocate them a random passer-by. Each pair was instructed to follow their random person for a minimum of 15 minutes, and to return to our office within 30 minutes. There are certain safety and security implications doing this exercise in a live environment but we generally operated in an upmarket business or shopping district that was very busy and generally safe. The participants of the course had every right to be in the area; two friends or colleagues taking a stroll before heading back to a meeting. There was nothing illegal about what they were doing. They were briefed to abort if there was the slightest chance that they had attracted attention from the authorities, or if they were walking to an area they weren't comfortable, or if the target became suspect that he or she was being followed; it was of paramount importance that they did not unnerve anyone.

In the debrief following this exercise almost every team said that they had felt very self-conscious and exposed. They found it hard to get too close to the target, although some did, but only to break away quite quickly. Only one pair ever came back stating that they thought the exercise was a waste of time; that it was too easy to follow someone; they did not feel nervous and could not understand why the other teams felt that way.

We probed a little deeper and asked exactly what they had done, where they had gone, what distancing they used. They had followed at quite a distance, and the target just walked for ten minutes and then entered a high street bank.

We asked why they followed at such a great distance compared to the other teams. The answer was that they did not want to be seen and weren't comfortable being so close. We asked what the target did in the bank; did they work there, did they have a meeting, did they pay in money or withdraw? The reply was "We didn't go into the bank because there was a guard and we didn't want to be seen".

So, although the team said they could not relate to their peers about nervousness and exposure, they did not feel the nervousness and exposure because they were too nervous and feeling exposed to do the task properly!

If you do conduct such an exercise, for safety and control purposes it is better if the person you allocate a team to follow is actually someone you know who is purposefully there. That way you can get feedback from the target as well: how close the team got, whether they were noticed and if they raised suspicion. It also means that there is no member of the public who should be concerned that they are being followed.

Exercise 4 - Route Planning

As a table-top exercise you can take a routine that you use, such as leaving home and going to the office, and with the use of maps you can work out alternative routes than the one you generally take, and see if any of them are safer. Are they going through nicer neighbourhoods, are there safe havens on the journey, is there a hospital nearby for emergency medical assistance? Is there anything on your route that is clearly a choke point that could be used to ambush you? Are there points along your route where you can divert to another route if there are traffic problems or to change up the routine?

Exercise 5 - Planning an Attack

Another table-top exercise that you can do as a small group, or several small groups, is to plan the kidnap of one of your group. The one tasked as being the victim will be asked by the other members of the group about their routine over the course of a week. They then must work out where to conduct the kidnap with the highest probability of success.

This type of exercise is beneficial for everyone. People see how much routine there really is in their day to day lives and they also understand which locations an attacker might deem a good choke point.

This exercise can be 30 minutes long or you can go into much more detail and spend hours. The idea though is not to plan—or execute—an actual kidnap but just to demonstrate the potential weak spots in your routines so that you can protect yourself better.

Exercise 6 – Surveillance Detection Route

As mentioned in the *Detecting Surveillance* chapter of the *Kidnap Prevention* section, you can set up a Surveillance Detection Route. This is not something that you are likely to spend time setting up unless you have a situation you are aware of or you are a person at risk and you want to conduct random counter-surveillance.

For either reason, it is a good idea to practise doing it before you conduct one for real, so that you are familiar with the method. The best learning is always done through "real" practice.

I won't repeat here how to plan the SDR because you have already learnt about it in the *Kidnap Prevention* section so please refer back there for the information you need.

It should be clear that this is a sensitive topic so only use people you can trust who are mature, stable and responsible. They should not put themselves in danger and they need to be covert and surreptitious in their conduct, and act completely relaxed and normal so as not to draw attention to themselves.

Whether you have one person or three people as counter-surveillance helping you, do not forget that if you are conducting a training session that it is preferable to bring in one or two "suspicious" people to actually follow you. This gives your counter-surveillance team something tangible to look out for. Whether or not you tell them that you have people following you is up to you.

After the first run you can all meet up at a particular location (not the places where you conducted the exercise!) and debrief. See if your counter-surveillance people saw anything suspicious. Then bring in (if you have not done so already) the "suspicious" people you had following you and let them say where they were, what they did and what they observed. This all helps with the overall learning. You can then run the exercise again. The followers can change their appearance (coats, hats, glasses) or for example can walk holding hands instead of apart. You can play with it however you like.

Epilogue

I hope you have enjoyed reading this book and found it informative; that it has opened your eyes to the types of attacks you could be faced with, and the kind of situations you can find yourself in. People who participated in our original course usually came out of it pretty much shell shocked. They had in essence been forced to realise that the world is not a safe place; their collective heads pulled out of the sand; the bubble of denial protecting them from the frightening reality had burst. That sounds harsh, but it was a necessary part of the process because they were in places of very high risk.

Hopefully after reading this book your levels of paranoia have elevated and you are now super aware of everything going on around you. You will see a "mugger" behind every corner, "kidnappers" hiding in dustbins, "rapists" following you in the darkened streets waiting for an opportunity to attack you, and "street thugs" eyeing you up looking for a fight. But don't worry. After a few days this "fear" will dissipate, and in its place you will simply be left with a heightened sense of awareness.

I thank you for purchasing this book and truly hope it helps to keep you safe. If you have any security or self protection questions, or have any incidents that you would like to share, especially if they tie in with aspects of this book, please feel free to email me.

Keep safe, Oscar

www.oscarleon.uk.com

13511139R00103

Printed in Great Britain
by Amazon.co.uk, Ltd.,
Marston Gate.